DEATH TO LIFE: BANGLADESH

As Experienced by a Missionary Family

by

Jim McKinley

Publisher:

The Highview Baptist Church

Bill Hancock, Pastor

Selling Agent:

The Highview Baptist Church

7711 Fegenbush Lane

Louisville, Kentucky 40228

The book is available in lots of fifty only

Printer:

Courier-Journal Lithographing Co., Inc.

Louisville, Kentucky 40218

D1433074

DEDICATION

To Betty, Cherie, Kathy, Keith and Wade
who were soldiers of love
in the midst of deep suffering
and
To our Bengali friends who suffered
and often continue to suffer
in the struggle of their beautiful country.

FOREWORD

This book is a heart-rending and heart-warming account of Bengali suffering and desperate heroism during natural disaster and war, of friendship and relief for needy people, of "doing the gospel" of Jesus Christ, and of agony, love, unity, and growth in a missionary family. The time is the thirteen months preceding the birth of Bangladesh in December of 1971.

James F. McKinley and his wife, Betty, are among Southern Baptists' most capable and most faithful missionaries. His colleagues in Bangladesh (formerly East Pakistan) have repeatedly demonstrated their confidence in him by electing him their chairman. During years of living among the Bengalis the McKinleys have come to love them dearly. When tidal waves and floods came, they became heavily involved in relief and rehabilitation. When civil war broke out and most foreigners left the country, they decided to remain with their children among their Bengali friends.

Why would the Foreign Mission Board permit missionaries to remain in a war zone? It certainly does not require them to do so and fully supports those who decide to leave. It was better not to have a large staff of missionaries in East Pakistan during the civil war. However, missionaries on the scene are often in a better position than Foreign Mission Board administrators to decide what to do in a crisis situation; and the Foreign Mission Board usually does not order them to leave their adopted home-land. Jim felt that he should stay with the Bengalis and that he could if he had his family with him; Betty and the children decided to remain.

What was the effect on the children? They came through the ordeal unscathed physically and also, so far as we can see, emotionally. The whole family seems to be better rather than worse — with greater appreciation of life, new dimensions of Christian commitment, and enhanced love and unity.

Good missionaries always identify with the people among whom they live and work. During the civil war, in groups that might have been hostile to most Americans, Jim repeatedly heard the words, "He is one of us." When I began reading his manuscript I became a bit afraid that he had violated the Foreign Mission Board's counsel to its missionaries that they be politically neutral so that the gospel can be offered to people of all political persuasions. My fear was unjustified. Though Jim was very sympathetic with the Bengalis' struggle for justice and freedom, and was tempted to hate those who killed Bengalis and drove them from their homes, he never became a freedom fighter, a spy, or even a propagandist. Another book could be written about how, after Bengali freedom was achieved, the hearts and hands of the McKinleys and their colleagues went out in love to needy people on the losing side. It would probably be correct to say that their sympathies are always with those most in need.

Jim McKinley is a great relief worker, but that is not his main interest. He is a missionary evangelist, and he is happiest when he is engaged in evangelism and church development. He did not lose heart when there was little response to the gospel. Now he has the joy of seeing many people, especially in villages, becoming interested in Christ and not a few accepting Him as Savior and Lord and becoming church members.

The McKinleys and their colleagues need help. May many readers of this book become helpers in Bangladesh, and may some become missionary evangelists.

J. D. Hughey

Secretary for Europe, the Middle East, and South Asia
The Foreign Mission Board
of the Southern Baptist Convention

PREFACE

This is a story of a missionary family, my family, who lived in its adopted land through a thirteen month period of suffering created by natural and man-made disasters.

Soon after the liberation of Bangladesh, I was told by friends that I should write the story in full detail. I had many notes which I had kept during the period of suffering, but since I had done very little formal writing, I neglected the opportunity for a long time.

Then, Mr. Bob Terry, who was with the Western Recorder, the Kentucky Baptist paper, asked me to write a series of articles. Those articles appeared in seven consecutive weekly editions. They were well accepted so this was an encouragement to me. Soon, some of the same material appeared in the The Commission, the magazine of the Foreign Mission Board of the SBC.

I find myself today grateful to Mr. Terry, Dr. Daley, Editor of the Western Recorder, and to Dr. North, editor of The Commission for their support in sharing experiences that mean much to me and my family.

Other friends eventually helped me by typing the manuscript. They include Mrs. Milon Majunder of Bangladesh, Mrs. Lealia Gentle and Mrs. Delta Felts of Louisville, Kentucky.

Mrs. Carl Williams volunteered to work hard and long in trying to make the manuscript readable. She attempted to take my awkward English and come up with something satisfactory and at the same time to preserve my style. The faults of the book are mine, not hers, since she made every effort to let me speak in my way. She knows me for she was my teacher for seven years and my senior class sponsor in high school.

Dr. and Mrs. Wayne Ward of Southern Seminary in Louisville insisted from the time they read the first rough manuscript that I stay with the task. I appreciate them for doing this.

The long list of beautiful friends continues with Miss Carolyn Weatherford who read the manuscript during the meeting of the Southern Baptist Convention in Atlanta and wrote a recommendation for the book.

You cannot find a person with more important things to do than Mr. Owen Cooper but he took time to read the manuscript and write a recommendation. No one is more qualified to do this than Mr. Cooper.

And could you imagine — during the meeting of the Southern Baptist Convention in Atlanta, I built up enough courage to ask Mrs. Jimmy Allen to read the manuscript and give a note of encouragement for the book. She did it at a time when her husband was presiding over the meeting of the Southern Baptist Convention as President.

Dr. and Mrs. Ward, Mr. Cooper and Mrs. Allen have been in Bangladesh as our guests. They have seen the people about whom I have written.

Several students at Southern Seminary read the manuscript and said, "Hang in, Jim." So, I hung in and the book is ready for the press and I hope for thousands of people who will read it and give thanks to God for his mercy in the midst of suffering.

This long list of friends could go on and on but the person who perhaps means most to me and my family in our missionary ministry is Dr. J. D. Hughey, of the Foreign Mission Board, who is a faithful friend and our "Boss" for several years. "Thanks" is not enough for his writing of the foreword and associating himself with the book.

As you read, please remember that you have made a contribution to the people who suffered and made this book possible. The Foreign Mission Board has permitted me to say that all profits from the book will go to Bangladesh for special projects. The book doesn't belong to me nor to the beautiful friends who have supported it but it belongs to the ones who suffered.

Highview Baptist Church of Louisville, Kentucky must now do the work. They have accepted the responsibility for publishing and selling the book. They will send the profit from sales to the Foreign Mission Board for use in Bangladesh.

Pastor Bill Hancock and Highview have accepted another ministry of love and I thank them for it.

The book thrusts the reader into suffering with the first line and it concludes abruptly with the liberation of the world's eighth largest country in population.

No attempt was made to be technical with the references to war and the names of many groups involved in the struggle of Bangladesh. I simply called all of those who fought for the liberation of their country "Freedom Fighters".

Finally, please permit me to say that I am not a person of any great faith but my family and I found that God gives faith — enough for the time along with His grace. We experience more of both daily as we move along in the struggle of life.

Jim McKinley
Box 99
Dacca 2, Bangladesh

CHAPTER ONE

Kathy, my eleven year old daughter, came running into the house screaming. "Daddy! Daddy!" she cried in distress; "planes are coming!"

Betty, my wife, and I ran with her to the back door. We saw two jet fighters of the Pakistan Air Force sweeping across the rice fields at low altitude. In seconds, they neared our house which was located west of the little border town of Feni in what was then East Pakistan.

In the direction of the planes, our thirteen year old daughter, Cherie, was chasing down her two brothers, Keith age seven and Wade age five. Keith and Wade were too young to understand the danger of the on-coming planes. But Cherie remembered the previous warning I had given them about the possible danger. She knew those low swift movements meant trouble.

She grabbed her little brothers and pulled them down to earth. The planes zoomed over them spewing bullets by the hundreds. Betty, Kathy and I looked on in horror. The rattling of the shooting guns roared out with earth splitting sounds. I rubbed my ears seeking relief. Screams of agony and death echoed out across the rice fields as bullets found their mark in the bodies of our Bengali friends and neighbors.

As the planes passed over, I ran to Cherie, Keith and Wade to bring them into the house — our place of "Security."

"Oh, God, what now?" recked my brain. We were in our thirteenth year as missionaries in East Pakistan. We had seen tragedy on many occasions but never anything like this. Now we were caught in the midst of civil war between the military forces of West Pakistan and the people of East Pakistan.

1

We huddled in the narrow hallway of our house, frozen in fear, as the planes made five more strikes upon the unarmed citizens of our little town.

Sultan, our Muslim cook, began screaming and rolling in the floor.

Bablu, our little Muslim neighbor boy, was also caught with us. He lay quivering on the floor. Kathy called to him, "Bablu, pray to God. I know He will help us."

Noren, our Hindu helper, was no less distressed. Keith looked to him and said, "Noren, don't be afraid; God will save us."

But this was fleeting faith, for the children were soon asking, "Daddy, Daddy, what will happen to us? Will we all be killed?" My assurance was weak. I only answered, "We will manage somehow."

The pilots of those planes were successful if the slaughter of defenseless human beings can be called success. But they were not content with this attack alone. As they departed, we heard guns burst forth on a rural market nearby. More innocent people ate the lead from the planes and died.

After reassuring the children that everything was okay for the time being, I ran down the road to the main street of Feni. As I ran, soft little words trailed after me, "Daddy, Daddy, hurry back." By this time, hundreds of people were fleeing the town. They raced down the road and across the fields carrying the dead and dying. Our children had been miraculously saved but not the hundreds of others. Friends called out to me, "Go back, they will kill you, too."

The main street was jammed with cycle rickshaws, bullock carts and people crying out for family members and friends. To most of them; there was only one thought — to get out of town immediately before those planes had time to return and bring more death.

But a few brave men were able to control themselves. One of these, Khawja Ahmed, a leading politician and a newly elected member of the National Assembly, organized and cared for the wounded. Men carried torn bodies to the little twenty-five bed hospital. Through the years, this hospital had served an area of 600,000 people and was often without a surgeon. Now it faced its greatest challenge.

A Bengali young man helped me place an elderly gentleman on a long table. His left leg was bent under his body. Shattered, protruding bones tore through his flesh. He was dying. We carried him to the little hospital. One man who had lost all emotional control cried out to me, "Look, look!" I looked at the body of a man whose head had been split open with a line of bullets.

Feni is a country town. Though the population is over 15,000, it is little more than a large market place. Most of the people who fill the streets on the special market days are nearby villagers. They come to buy and to sell. A majority of them are illiterate. On market days hundreds of them can be seen on all the streets selling and buying. This day, April 6, 1971, was a big market day. The streets were jammed with people, cows, and wares of every fashion. The bullets had no difficulty in finding human flesh to tear and human bones to break.

Prior to the brutal plane attack, most of the people knew about the foreign family who lived among them. And most of them knew we were Christian missionaries, though they did not know us by name. Often they inquired about our work. Some of them had difficulty understanding why we had left a rich country to live with them. Slowly, since our first arrival in Feni in January, 1965, we had seen some of that lack of understanding erased. At times, we felt many of our neighbors had accepted us.

But now there was no doubt. We were part of them. We were all caught in the same death trap. Their newly elected popular national leader had declared a few days earlier that the friends of Bengalis were considered Bengalis. This was a graciously wide umbrella, and it certainly covered us.

One frantic man looked at me, grabbed my arm and cried out, "Oh, Sir, we are so glad you are with us."

Brave men carried dozens of bodies, torn into shreds, into the hospital. Many others, however, screaming and irrational, carried their dead and dying across the countryside. Most of them had no choice but to die without treatment.

Suren Sircar's little girl disappeared during the deathly disruption. The next day a village man brought her home. She had followed the crowd into the country, and no one had courage enough to return her that night.

But as always, there was some comfort in the midst of the greatest distress. I walked through the hospital looking for those I might recognize. One man, whose leg had been shot off just below the knee, called out to me. I stood by his bedside. He held my hand and rubbed my arm. He was a local Communist leader. Today there were no shouts against the local "American dogs" as the Communist often called us.

3

Then a more familiar voice called out, "Sahib, Sahib", meaning sir, "come to me." It was Dhanu Mia, a cycle rickshaw operator. Many times I had ridden in his rickshaw, and often he had said, "You should never pay me; you are our guest." Of course, I always paid him because earning a living was most difficult for a poor man. But his attitude had always given me a lift.

Today Dhanu Mia's voice was weak, but he appeared to be okay. When he threw back the sheet, I knew, however, that he had operated his last rickshaw. A line of bullets had torn off his left foot. "Dhanu Mia," I said, "we will help you get some kind of job when your foot has healed. You have friends, and all of us will help you."

Dhanu Mia was a large Bengali. He stretched his big arms toward me. I bent over him. His strong arms pulled me tightly to his chest. He gripped me. For a few moments there was silence. There was no doubt; this Bengali Muslim loved his Christian missionary friend. "I'll see you tomorrow," was all I had to say. And I said that without thinking of what that would bring.

I walked out of the hospital sopping the tears away. What else could I do but weep and hope and pray? Outside the hospital a poorly dressed man ran up to me and said, "You won't leave us, will you?" Without thinking I answered, "No, I'll not leave you."

Others came carrying hands full of bullets which had struck brick buildings and fallen to the earth. One man with trembling hands showed me his collection, shook his head, and walked away silently. After the first thirty minutes or so passed, most people were numb with silence.

Thinking of those hands filled with bullets, I walked back toward the house. I no longer wondered about the destruction that bullets bring when fired. I now knew what they did to human flesh and bones. Night was approaching, but I walked slowly. This was my opportunity to think. What was I to do in this "hell on earth" where I was caught with my family. My quiet was disturbed as I walked along the road. One man said, "Sir, watch the sky. More planes may come. Walk fast."

Betty and the children were waiting by the roadside in front of our house. They had witnessed the exodus of a few thousand people in that short time. Our children had learned early in life the inhumanity of man to man!

Since our house was west of Feni, most of the people went in that direction. The road out of Feni to the North ran along the

4

nearby Indian border. The road to the East was even nearer the border; and the one to the South was used by several people, but ours was the main road of Noakhali District and her 3,000,000 people.

That road showed us much human suffering in a short time. There had been a complete blackout in Feni ever since the civil war had broken out on March 25. But the night of April 6th was much quieter than the previous ones. All of Feni and the surrounding rural area faced darkness in a quiet fear.

Even the crickets disturbed my attempts to rest. The children, however, seemed to sleep well, and that was the thing that counted most. That night of contemplation sent my mind wondering about our situation. It led me to think that we were really on a hot spot. The main road of East Pakistan from Chittagong, the port city, ran through Feni and on to Dacca, the provincial capital. The main railway between these two cities also passed through Feni. Over the back corner of our yard was the high tension electric line running from East Pakistan's only dam to Dacca.

I knew nothing about war; but I knew that if fighting continued, we would be in the midst of it. Though I had never traveled the road because of its relationship to the Indian border, I knew there was a road to the east and then north of Feni which leads into India. A train track followed the same route. But regardless of our present situation, I considered myself an extremely fortunate man. I confess to great pride in my family. Ten years after our marriage, our first son was born. This was very important for a man in Pakistan.

To some it had seemed God had not favored me well since up to that time he had given me only two daughters. But now I had been highly favored — two sons after two daughters. But regardless of what others thought, I felt mine was a perfect family. Betty had given herself to us being mother — and far more. She was also the teacher of our children.

Then too, I had come close to being cut off from them when the civil war first broke out. Early on the morning of March 25, I went to Dacca with my missionary colleague, R. T. Buckley, who lived on the route to Dacca. We made the trip to talk with our Dacca missionaries about the seemingly dangerous situation. However since discussions were taking place by all those involved in the different political groups, our Dacca missionaries seemed to feel that everything was going to be settled without too much difficulty.

5

But just before lunch, R. T. and I traveled down Mirpur Road. Near the junction which led to the home of Sheik Mujibur Rahman, we saw several truck loads of heavily armed West Pakistani soldiers. Sheik Mujib had been elected as the new leader of Pakistan in the recent elections, but the military were unwilling to turn the governing power over to him until the demands of the other political leaders were met. In many areas of the country, Bengali civilians of East Pakistan had resisted the West Pakistani soldiers; and, as a result, many civilians had been killed. This had led Bengalis to attack others whose allegiance was to West Pakistan and her military forces. Many of those were Muslim Biharis who had come to East Pakistan when India was divided in 1947 and the new nation, Pakistan, was created. The Biharis had initiative, and many of them were gifted at mechanical work. They were also good businessmen, so they made progress which was resented by many Bengalis.

But they had also been favored by the primarily West Pakistan controlled government since 1947. This had led Sheik Mujib to plead for peace among the civilians and for treatment to all as Bengalis. Each delay, however, in giving power to the newly elected government caused Bengalis to distrust all those related to West Pakistan. Chaos followed in the industrial areas especially since Bihari and West Pakistan civilians were largely involved in industry.

R. T. and I felt insecure in being so far away from our families after seeing that large number of armed soldiers near Sheik Mujib's home. We decided to have a quick lunch at the Hotel Intercontinental and hastily make our way back to Comilla and Feni. The hotel was filled with reporters who were loudly discussing all that was transpiring in the political discussions. But since all the meetings were closed to reporters, their guesses were only as good as ours. We ate hurriedly and moved back toward our homes and families.

A military base is located west of Comilla so we approached the area with some apprehension. Fortunately, though, as we turned on the interior lights, the soldiers motioned us on without question.

In Comilla, R. T. got down quickly. It was now about nine o'clock. and I had the forty mile border road to travel. But I made good time and was soon in Feni.

As soon as Betty saw me she asked, "Is there any trouble in Dacca?" I replied, "No, why?" Several Feni friends who knew I had gone to Dacca had called during the day to inquire about my return. They feared trouble and, as friends, wanted me with them.

6

Though we did not hear about it until the next morning, that night the West Pakistan military forces turned upon the Bengalis of East Pakistan in full force to subdue them. The Bengali members of the armed forces who did not escape were killed. Those who escaped formed the nucleus of the Freedom Fighters for the new nation which was to be called Bangladesh, the nation of the Bengalis.

In all the areas of East Pakistan, the Pakistan military forces moved with brute force to destroy the Bengali people and their culture. For me it was an almost unbelievable situation. However I should have known this was coming. I remembered that soon after the national elections, I had seen troop movements in areas never before noticed.

I recalled that even in our little town there were several soldiers on the northeastern side. I saw them one day when I took a new kind of specially made bricks for testing. Those bricks, if strong enough, were going to be used in the recent tidal wave disaster of our district. They were made mostly of clay but with a small amount of cement in them. A highly revered Bengali gentleman, Mr. Alam Chasi, had asked me to take them to this Bengali friend who lived in the northeastern part of Feni. But when I saw the soldiers that day, I thought nothing of it. I was on a mission of service not even thinking of the political events.

But on the morning of March 26, 1971, I was home with my family. We were surrounded by Bengali friends. So we were not anxious. We only waited to see but, in the meantime, continued our work as best we could.

Actually I felt quite secure. The highest government official in our area was Belal Khan, a West Pakistani. Since he did not speak Bengali, he was handicapped in his relationship with the people. But they seemed to like him. He had recently fought for and secured new street lights for the town. He was working on securing funds for a badly needed park and public meeting place. I supported him in these efforts and attended public meetings at his request.

When the attack of the Pakistan military forces began, Mr. Belal, of course, was in trouble. When the first meeting of the newly elected National Assembly was cancelled on March 3, 1971, it was assumed from that time on that all West Pakistanis were enemies of the people of Bangladesh. Every time I saw Mr. Belal after that date, he seemed very nervous.

But my family did not consider him an enemy of the Bengalis.

7

At one public meeting I attended, he invited both of the newly elected Feni members of the National Assembly to address the group; and it seemed they had a good relationship.

Because he feared the Bengalis, I felt we should befriend him even more. Since we had no fear of Bengalis, I was confident we could help him. Betty agreed for us to invite him for dinner even though some Bengalis might think we were friends of one of the enemy. Mr. Belal accepted the invitation after explaining that he needed to bring a friend with him. The friend was a West Pakistani, Captain Zia of the Pakistan Army. He was the Commander of the newly located group of troops in Feni, though at that time, I did not even consider why he was in Feni. I didn't even recall the presence of those troops.

Captain Zia came in civilian dress but was armed with a small pistol and another crude looking gun which he laid on a table. I later learned the second weapon was a deathly sten gun. He said, after laying the guns down, "My job is to protect Mr. Belal." I was embarrassed in the presence of my children, for I had invited a guest who believed weapons were necessary for safety. I did not own a weapon of any kind and had no desire for one.

The conversation around the table was dull at times, for we kept coming back to the political situation. Of course, our guests supported the General. My family felt that he should immediately turn the government over to Sheik Mujib and his Awami League Party which had easily won the national election.

Captain Zia was not as gentle as Mr. Belal. Once he blurted out, "We will drive the Bengalis back two centuries. We will kill as many as necessary." My children were disturbed by almost everything he said.

After all, they took pride in their long years in the land of the Bengalis. Cherie had arrived in East Pakistan when she was ten months old. Kathy and Keith were born there, and Wade arrived when he was three weeks old. Betty and the three older children were evacuated in the 1965 India-Pakistan War. They spent several months in the Philippines since Betty could not return because she was expecting Wade. But Wade was an early traveler. He left Manila and traveled to Hong Kong for a few days. Then, after an overnight stop in Bangkok, Thailand, he arrived in Dacca on his 21st day. The same day he went to Feni, one hundred miles from Dacca.

We were relieved when Mr. Belal and Captain Zia stood to

depart soon after eating. Mr. Belal was courteous as he left. He remarked, "Look, even I have a black flag on a jeep indicating that I am opposed to the killing of innocent civilians." I wasn't sure whether he was ridiculing or speaking truthfully. Maybe the black flag was there only to protect him from mobs on the highways. Captain Zia had little to say as he climbed into the jeep. We were relieved as they drove away.

Early the next morning after my return to Feni from Dacca, we learned of what was happening; for the Dacca radio station was still controlled by the Bengalis.

I decided to try to understand the situation. I knew Mr. Abdul Malek, the owner of a hardware store in downtown Feni, would share freely with me. Long before I had known that he was a politician, we had been friends. He had always been helpful to me as a foreigner. I also liked him because he, as a Muslim, had a Hindu employed in his store. I thought this always helped communal relationships; and since I was a member of a tiny religious minority, his support of the Hindus spoke to me.

While I sat in his little store, the telephone rang. I listened carefully and heard Mr. Malek say, "If you do not have enough dynamite, I can help you locate some. After he hung up the telephone, I asked, "Sir, what is happening?" "We are destroying all road and railway bridges to the North and South," he answered. "We must stop the movement of the army. If they come here, they will kill us all." This was a poor land. It was going to be poorer quickly, I thought. Bengalis were dying for their freedom. What was the importance of steel, brick and mortar?

The radio news gave a terrible picture of Dacca; we only guessed what was happening in other places.

But on March 27, we saw first hand the results of the army brutality. Thousands of people with swollen feet seemingly ready to burst open marched by our house. Their faces were marked with a deep fear. Their weapons were bamboo sticks. Many of them had no idea where they were going except that they were escaping the army. Most of them were fortunate to be alive; for they had come from the two large cities, Dacca and Chittagong, where the army had been most brutal.

Some had walked the entire distance of one hundred miles from Dacca. Day and night they had plodded along, hoping to reach families and friends. Those coming from Chittagong had walked sixty-five miles, and they had seen fighting all along the route. Safety was sought in the hills which followed the highway most of the distance. Many of them were going into the interior of our district, Noakhali. However some of those going north were trying to reach families in Comilla and Sylhet Districts. The children watched them for long hours as they passed by in a steady stream. It hurt to watch.

The Bengalis are a peaceful people. Even the police did not usually carry weapons. Most men had never held a gun in their hands, much less fired one. The planes, tanks and automatic weapons of the army had demoralized them. Most appeared subdued. It seemed there was no strength left to walk; certainly there was none to fight a well equipped army. They wanted to live and be left in peace. But now that was not a simple desire.

There were encouraging signs, however. As the refugees struggled along the roads, farmers set up little food stands offering milk, green coconut juice, and other food from their meager supply to help them. Everything was free. This was not the Bengali spirit I had previously witnessed. But I liked what I saw.

Our district was still open. The destroyed bridges had kept the army out. I was free to travel as necessary though fuel was at a premium. I spent several days driving back and forth along the main highway going east and west in front of our house. I limited the number of passengers to twelve except when it meant breaking up a family. Each time as I stopped to turn back, I called out for twelve passengers.

Sometimes, in desperation for a ride, they overloaded the vehicle. I asked them to get down. They got out of the car apologizing for overloading it. I discovered in talking with these fleeing people that something had really happened to them. They were not subdued as I had thought. They had been driven together by an angry army. Though I had times of doubt about the possibility of independence, I felt that the army had gone too far. It had driven the Bengalis to a fight for independence or death.

I suppose Noakhali could have been called a little "nation." We had our own government. I never had second thoughts about giving them full cooperation.

Soon after March 25th, village leaders in our area came to say, "We had a meeting and organized ourselves into groups to protect our homes. We did not invite you since it might have appeared a political meeting. But we want you and your family to be assured that your home will be protected along with ours." They informed us of the man responsible for our protection.

This gave us new assurance. It also caused us to think about what the army would do when it did arrive in Feni. Would there be questions as to how we had been able to live peaceably when our district was under "rebel" control? We were cooperating with the "rebels", but this was our choice — not our only alternative. We could have crossed the border into India, or we could have moved toward army controlled territory. But it seemed only natural to cooperate with the people among whom we had lived. They were our friends. If we could not live with them and work with them, then our reason for being in Pakistan was invalid.

I did have fears. A few months earlier I had, with the help of government officers, asked a group of students to move their meeting from the front of our evangelistic office. They had, without my consent, started their meeting during the time our office was closed for lunch. I understood they were a political organization and explained that we could not be related to any political group. They were embarrassed when they had to close their meeting. One of the student leaders had declared that he would "get me." Now he had an excellent opportunity. We had no police force, for our police had moved across the border into India to flee the army. Since they were the first to be attacked in other areas, it was only natural for them to leave.

I was greatly relieved when a superior of the student, whom I felt was my enemy, came and said, "Do not be afraid for yourself or your family. Nothing will happen to you."

A leftist newspaper had attacked me on two occasions calling me a spy. This would be an opportunity for them to cause us real difficulty. However the editor came to the house only to seek my opinion about what the army would do when it reached Feni.

Some years earlier, a rightwing fanatical Muslim had threatened me and declared he would burn our evangelistic office. Now he felt that we were brothers.

We felt that we belonged. There is a degree to which this may seem unusual. We, a white missionary family, living among Muslims and Hindus who were dark skinned, felt a real part of the community. Our purpose was to preach the good news of Jesus. We made no apology for this. Everyone knew that we were there to win people to Christ or, as they would say, "to make converts." Yet they claimed us and we liked that.

11

Though I had fears because of my involvements, I do not think there was ever a time when our children even thought about fearing any of the Bengalis in our area. This was the Bengalis' home. This was our home. I always chose to believe that our children felt united with the people against the army.

At night we lay in bed and watched the sky being lighted with the firing of what were apparently huge guns. The ocean was nearly twenty miles away. We assumed the firing was from ships. The constant roar of the guns was alarming, but it seemed far away.

Most Bengalis with whom we talked in Feni felt that the army would never reach there. Reports were coming in saying that the Freedom Fighters of Bangladesh were putting up strong resistance and would eventually win. I doubted this would be soon since, when I was downtown, I rarely ever saw anyone with weapons; and when I did, those weapons seemed to be obsolete. On the other hand, it appeared the army was well equipped and well trained.

The refugees passing through Feni kept telling the stories of horror. Fear began mounting. The contingent of Pakistan soldiers in Feni became the main topic of discussion. When would those soldiers turn upon the civilians in Feni? Why had they not already done it? Then it became apparent. They were cut off from all other units and did not know what was happening. It was also discovered that the Bengali soldiers in this group had not escaped but were being held by the West Pakistanis as prisoners in a large building. Stories circulated saying that some of the Bengali soldiers had been killed in their first attempt to escape.

The Bengali civilians decided to attack the West Pakistani forces hoping to rescue the Bengali soldiers and take the Pakistanis as prisoners. They soon discovered, however, that this was not an easy task. They had few and inferior weapons. They repeatedly asked me to go and watch the battle. But I had no desire to see anyone killed anywhere.

One young government officer came by the house and shared his story of what was happening. "I was walking toward the building the soldiers were using as a fortress. My friend walking by my side was shot down. I tried to lift him, but I was so afraid; all I could do was fall down and tremble." He continued, "Mr. McKinley, I want our freedom, but it does not seem that I will be a good fighter." I admired him. He was honest. Most of those with whom I talked were heroes after the battle was over. They did not say how they felt when they were in danger.

The best I could understand, most of the soldiers, Bengali and West Pakistani, died in the building. Many Bengali civilians died. We were told that Captain Zia's body was left for the dogs to devour. Approximately a month before, he had boasted of what he would do to the Bengalis. My prayer was, "God save us from hatred, from domination of others, and from war which leads to death. Somehow help us to find love for all men."

The temperament of our town changed. Soldiers were reportedly moving in from the South. Truck loads of civilians were transported out to meet them. The Pakistani soldiers dug in around a road and railway bridge about fifteen miles from Feni. They fought for several days. The Bengalis won. The two bridges were destroyed so that other soldiers coming in would have no means of crossing the river.

But every time a soldier died, many civilians died. Then on April 6th, the planes attacked. This changed everything. No one could challenge them. Morale was broken. Fears deepened. Friends came to our house saying, "Please do not leave, but be here with us when the army attacks." Our presence appeared to be a symbol of hope to many. Maybe that is why we were there. We did our best, however, to warn them that the army would not consider our presence when they attacked.

I expected the army to attack in force at any time. I told our children that when I saw the army approaching, I would walk out into the road so they could see I was a foreigner. God must protect the naive. Later the village people near our house said that the army killed everyone in sight when they marched into Feni. My debt to God grew daily.

I went to the hospital early the morning of April 7th to visit my friend Dhanu Mia. The hospital was closed. All of the patients had been moved to the interior for safety as well as to provide more space for the wounded.

But Dhanu Mia was dead. The previous afternoon no one had told me that his stomach was also filled with bullets. He died the first night. I had to do something. But what? I took some blankets and the money I thought we could spare to his wife and six children.

It became more difficult for our children to study. Betty taught them, but with all of the uncertainty, they could not concentrate. They continued to ask, "Daddy, what are we going to do?" Sooner or later, Feni would be attacked by the army.

Three times I sent young men to Comilla to try to find out something about the Buckleys. Fran Buckley was recovering from hepatitis, and their house was in the center of the town. We felt that the situation for them must be terrible. Though they had no way of knowing it, their presence in Comilla would influence us in making a decision concerning our departure from Feni. If Fran were quite sick, they might need our help. Each time, the young men reported, they had been unable to enter Comilla because of the army curfew.

At about 12:30 p.m., Friday, April 9th, Feni took another brutal beating by the Pakistan planes. They made seven strikes against the civilians. This time the attacks were made directly from over the house. It seemed the planes would touch the electric lines as they came in. The split second they were over our house, they released the bullets.

As soon as they had made their "impression", I ran down to the main street filled with anger and maybe even a touch of hatred for the pilots of those planes. Like "brave" men, they had killed without any danger of being killed. There was no way to challenge them. Again no one knew the number killed or wounded. A few bodies were taken to the little hospital. But most of them were carried to the country side by friends and relatives.

The planes had chosen an excellent time to strike. Many men had gathered in town because this was the time of day for prayers at the mosques. Strange as it may sound, one of the larger mosques had been the target of rockets from the planes. Bullets had riddled the office of the Imam on top of the mosque, and one rocket had landed just behind the pulpit. Though many of the orthodox Muslims later collaborated with the army, that day they were foaming with anger. One Muslim leader, to whom I had spoken many times but who always refused to speak to me, asked, "Sir, is Islam divided?" My reply was simple, "I do not know that answer. I only know that what is happening here is horrible."

Bengali guards protected the shops from looters. There was an effort to make things appear somewhat normal, but those planes had even altered expressions on faces. In a short time entire families were seen moving out of Feni. Friends who had earlier said, "Please do not leave us," were leaving. One bank manager embarrassingly asked, "Would you please take my family to a village home?" He was one of those who had pleaded for us to remain. Many friends asked, "Where will you go?" We did not know.

After the first strike by the planes, I had asked an American

14

engineer, who had been caught by the war while involved in bridge construction near Feni, to take Betty and the children to India with him. He agreed if they would be ready in a short time.

I felt that going into the hills of India at night would be too dangerous, so I asked him to wait until morning. He didn't think it safe to remain in Feni, so he departed a short time later. But his going helped, because he gave us time to write three letters: One to Betty's mother, and one to my parents and another one to Dr. Hughey at the Foreign Mission Board in Richmond, Virginia. He also took a cable which we requested him to send as soon as possible. The cable said, "Saw McKinley's in Feni; they are well." As he left, we asked him, "Please tell everything you have seen here. Do not worry about what will happen to us." He was faithful to us, for we learned weeks later that the letters and cable arrived.

I think Keith and Wade would have done anything their mother and I suggested. But with Cherie and Kathy, it was different. They, too, were considering the alternatives. They began saying, "Daddy, we must leave Feni."

A newly elected member of the Provincial Assembly of East Pakistan came by and asked us to go to his village about fifteen miles from the border. He offered to move his family to another house and give us his. His offer was gracious, but accepting it might have created even greater difficulties. He was a member of the Awami League Party which the army had outlawed. We had to decline.

Saturday morning, April 10th, we drove thirty miles west to the Canadian Catholic Mission. This proved to be a good decision. Sister Stella was a source of encouragement to Cherie and Kathy. Father Timm, with whom I played softball in Dacca soon after our first arrival in East Pakistan in 1958, had been "caught" there at the mission. He played ball with the boys and me. Our Catholic friends seemed to understand fully our difficulty concerning the children.

Returning to Feni from the Catholic mission, one of the children kept his head out the window all of the time watching for planes. We knew anything could be expected from those vultures of the sky.

I had committed myself to do everything possible to help relieve the people of our district from the tragedy of the cyclonic tidal wave of November 12th and 13th of 1970.

Soon after the war began, I visited an area about sixty-five miles southwest of our home. The Peter McNees of the New Zealand Baptist Mission were living in the area helping with the building of a model village. I felt some responsibility to the McNees since they had learned about this work, at least indirectly, from me. I had taken Mrs. McNee and their two sons to this area in my vehicle some weeks earlier.

I also felt a close relationship to the people who had suffered this great tragedy and to the other Bengalis who had gone there to help. Among those in Char Alexander at that time was a former Pakistan government foreign service member. Of all Bengalis I had come to know during the previous thirteen years, I had the deepest respect for Mr. Alam. He had left foreign service to come home and help his people develop their own land rather than beg food from foreign nations.

Before the planes struck Feni, I drove to Char Alexander. The dedication of the Bengali people became clearer to me. I learned that the previous day Mr. Alam and others had led a large group of men to a wide river channel near the ocean to face an oncoming ship which they understood to be loaded with Pakistan soldiers. They had gone to face what they thought were trained military men, and their only weapons were bamboo sticks. To their relief, however, it was a rebel ship loaded with Bengali refugees coming into Noakhali District. In the conversation with Mr. Alam, I discovered that these men went to face the ship knowing that most of them would be killed but that they would at least offer some resistance so that the Bengali women and children could escape. Though I thought they had done a foolish thing, my respect for Mr. Alam deepened. He could have easily been living in luxury in Peking, Moscow, Paris, London or Washington. His challenge left me with no other choice but to question my dedication to my Lord and to the people of this land.

Mr. Alam rode forty-five miles back toward Feni with me and the vehicle load of refugees. Near Maijdi he got down. A few days later he came to Feni. We visited briefly. Later I met with him and other leaders in Maijdi, our district headquarters, to discuss the possibility of continuing relief work in the disaster area. I had money which friends had given to me, so we agreed that as long as there was money and it was physically possible, we would continue relief work.

Perhaps it was all naive, but we made a long trip to visit another of the disaster areas and discussed what we could do in the present circumstances. I planned to get permission to take a

16

large sum of money from the bank for the proposed work. But the Pakistan planes changed all of our plans.

Mr. Alam visited again with us in Feni. Then he disappeared. Much later, good news came. Mr. Alam had become the Foreign Secretary of the Bangladesh government in exile in India. During the following weeks when I awakened at night, I often wondered what had happened to our good friend. I assumed, due to my lack of faith, that he had been killed by the army.

After the attack by the planes, I visited the McNees on two other occasions at night. I felt that Betty and our children might leave at any time, and I wanted the McNees to be aware of what we were doing. It was apparent that we could not continue living in Feni. One night, on my way back to Feni while traveling on the dirt section of the road, a Bengali walked out in front of me with a bamboo stick as his weapon. When I stopped, he recognized me. I rebuked him for what he had done, explaining that had my vehicle been a military vehicle, the soldiers would have killed him. He smiled and said, "Yes, they would have killed me, but look." Another man with his hand on a siren walked out of the bushes. "Had you been in a military vehicle, he would have sounded the siren, and dozens of men armed with bamboo would have been upon you." I apologized for my rudeness and drove toward home. "Maybe the Bengalis will be free," I thought.

The road leading east toward Feni was blocked about every five miles. At times I had difficulty identifying myself. Eventually I discovered that when I reported myself as the Bible man from Feni, the Bengali guards understood. We had six Bible centers in the district and hundreds of Bible students living in even the remote areas. I reached home at daybreak. It was always good to hear the screams from the children, "Mother, Daddy is home." We were in this thing together.

The second attack by the planes had taken place on Good Friday. One of the two Christian families in Feni had fled to India. The mother and older daughters of the other family were not in Feni, so on Easter Sunday, April 11th, our small band of Christians gathered at our regular place for worship. Death had covered East Pakistan, but was there hope for all people?

Monday afternoon, April 12th, after the children had completed their school work, we visited with a distinguished Bengali family about eight miles east of Feni. Mr. Abdur Rashid had retired as Secretary of Communications, Government of Pakistan, a few weeks earlier. He had brought his family to his village home.

17

The visit was pleasant and refreshing. We looked to Mr. Rashid for advice. He wisely had none to offer. He was wondering how he would ever get his family back to Dacca, where they were making their home. They had watched the plane attacks on Feni. He said to Betty, "Mrs. McKinley, it looked just like the many air shows we saw while we were serving in West Pakistan. We just could not believe it was real." Mr. Rashid turned to me and said, "Mr. McKinley, now all of us are poor people. We are all equal." I asked if there were something they especially needed. He replied, "Could you bring just a small amount of coffee for my wife?" It was apparent that his presence meant strength to many of the illiterate village people. He was known to them as a kind man.

Feni was becoming more desolate daily. One morning I was walking around casually speaking to friends when Professor Majumder called out to me, "Mr. McKinley, Mr. McKinley, wait, I must talk with you."

A few years earlier he had befriended me and perhaps saved my family from physical harm when some fanatical Muslims tried to disrupt our Bible teaching. Then just after he had been selected as one of the Awami League candidates for the National Assembly, he came to our house to ask for "my blessing." I told him that the best thing he could do was to stay completely away from me, even though we were friends, until after the election. I knew he did not need to be seen with me, a foreigner, since the accusation against me as a spy could also be used against him.

After the elections and his success, he came thanking me for the earlier advice. I gave him a book to read on the life of Sheik Mujibur Rahman, the leader of his party. He was seeking advice again. "What should I do? Where should my family go?" I did not hesitate. "You must get out of the country immediately with your family." I had no doubts. The members of the Awami League would be killed if caught by the army. He went to India.

Only a few men remained in Feni. It was now a ghost town. The shops were being guarded. As I walked through the empty streets, I could not help but recall the times of peace. Hundreds of Bengali men and boys had filled the streets as they walked to and from the villages with their wares. Now they huddled in nearby villages wondering what would happen next.

It became increasingly clear that we must also leave Feni. But leaving would not be easy. Feni was our home. Then, too, some of the survivors of the great cyclonic tidal wave of four and one-half months earlier depended upon me for help.

CHAPTER TWO

One-half million people had died in the coastal areas of East Pakistan in November, 1970. A local newspaper reported that two hundred thousand of these had died in our Noakhali District. And all this was just four and one-half months before the civil war began. Regardless of the difficulties my family might have to endure, I had to consider the people we would be leaving behind.

There was no need to be naive. Bengalis had endured great tragedies long before I was born. They no doubt would experience others long after I passed off the scene. But that did not relieve me of my responsibility to make their suffering a little easier at the time of the civil war.

Between October, 1960 and October, 1970, ten tidal waves had struck the coastal areas killing an estimated two hundred thousand people. The Bengalis of this area had been neglected. Something should have been done about an adequate warning system. The cost of one jet fighter would have more than covered the expense.

I suppose this tragedy made me feel guilty. On October 23, 1970, we as a family left Feni for Dacca enroute to Malaysia for a vacation. That day and part of the next, we were caught between two rivers without food or water for twenty-six hours. Fear struck. That night, after we had put all of our luggage on the floor of the vehicle, had piled bricks around the wheels, and had prayed for safety, Kathy cried out to Betty, "Mother, I am afraid." Betty replied, "But, Kathy, we have done all we know to do. You pray and ask God to help you rest." Kathy's reply was, "I have already done that twice."

Though we had to leave our vehicle because of the destroyed docks, we did make it into Dacca the following day. As we entered

19

the city, it was evident that the storm had been severe. Our flight the previous afternoon had not been able to land, so we made plans for the next one out.

The thirteenth of November we flew back to Dacca. Had we looked out the windows carefully, we could have seen the water from the Bay of Bengal flowing out of the coastal area. The previous night just before midnight, a killing wave of water swept across this, one of the world's most densely populated and least developed areas.

Death alone describes the results of this wave of water. Some claim that in the immediate coastal area the wave was thirty feet high. All I can say is — it must have been!

In one area the water came up a river channel. Then it gushed across the level rice fields without giving any attention to hundreds of little houses. An earthen dam caught this water and tried to turn it back toward the river. This only made the water swirl, tearing apart the little houses that had not already been ripped to pieces.

One side of the earthen dam was left undisturbed or at least, in the area where it was able to stop the water. The other side portrayed chaos. Rice straw was piled up several feet deep. For days men dug through the straw to find grains of rice which had fallen out. As they dug they found bodies — bodies of cattle, goats, chickens and human bodies puffed and stinking. Men worked with cloths tied over their mouths. Others stood nearby breathing moth balls to keep away the stench of death.

As my missionary companion, R. T. Buckley, and I drove south to look at the chaos, the number of bodies increased. After about ten miles down the dam, we had to turn back; for that mighty force of water had pushed aside tons of earth to make its own path.

We drove down the dam as doubters doubting that such a great tragedy had occurred. We commented that as we came back we would count the dead animals. It was not long until we lost all desire to count. The dead animals were too many, and who wanted to count the bodies of humans? We knew that regardless of what the outside world might be saying, death had struck and struck severely.

One week after the disaster, R. T. and I traveled to another area. We were preparing to put up a good plea for money to help in relief somewhere in Noakhali.

One group stopped up as we traveled deeper into the disaster

20

area. They demanded help immediately. We showed them the empty vehicle. It was only after this that they permitted us to proceed. Had we had anything in the vehicle, I am sure they would have taken it. Some men were becoming desperate.

We reached the coast of Noakhali District. Across the body of ocean water about ten miles away, Hatiya Island could be seen. We could only wonder how much they must have suffered. A tall dark-faced Bengali came toward us. "Come, let us show you everything," he said. Our quick reply was, "But we have nothing with which to help." To our surprise he said, "But we are not asking for help. Just come and walk with us." They offered us moth balls. We refused. We were missionaries; we could take it.

A few minutes later I was wishing for some of those moth balls. Why did I have to appear so pious? The stench of death was too much. We walked around the bodies on the earthen dam near the ocean. As the water had gushed in, it had destroyed parts of the dam. But destroying it was not necessary here. The wave was high enough to pour over the top to kill and devastate. Little villages inside the dam had been as brutally beaten as those outside. This had been a killer.

In most of the villages in the immediate coastal area, no one had survived. One survivor, a young man, however, joined our group as we walked. His bare chest had open bleeding wounds. He had climbed one of the palm trees. The stickers on the tree had torn his chest as he had clung on for his life. We asked, "But how did you endure the pain?" He answered, "I did not know there was any pain. I only wanted to live." As I looked about, I wondered, "Why?"

Relatives came into the area to claim the few remaining articles left in the villages. Approximately one hundred houses had stood around the bank of one little pond. The only thing left now was the slick surface of earth which had been the floor of the houses. No one had survived.

We prepared to leave saying, "Maybe we will be able to return, but most likely we will work in areas nearer to Feni." "That's okay," came the reply, "but we thank you for coming and walking with us and letting us tell you about what happened." And this tragedy happened while I had been on vacation.

Help — we must. But what? What could we do? We had no food. We could purchase clothing, but that was not the greatest need. We should do something that others could or would not immediately do. We made our offer to do whatever the local government officer suggested. "Could you put down tube wells?" he asked. "Yes, we can put down tube wells," I replied.

The procedure was simple. A small hole was dug. A simple wooden frame was placed over the hole. The workmen then placed a long one and one-half inch diameter galvanized pipe into the hole. A lever was attached to the pipe and to the wooden frame. One man climbed the frame and poured the pipe full of water. The water overflowed and filled the hole to cut off all air.

One man remained on the frame and placed the palm of his hand over the open end of the pipe. Another man pushed down on the lever lifting the pipe. He quickly released the lever, letting the pipe hit the bottom of the hole. Just as it hit, the man on top lifted the palm of his hand momentarily, letting the muddy earth squirt up through the pipe. The process was repeated rapidly. It was easy to watch the pipe sink down into the soil. Down there, usually about twenty-five feet, was safe drinking water. So the process of "sinking tube wells" began.

Why tube wells? Most of the area had been covered with the salty ocean water. The sources of water such as tanks and ponds had been contaminated not only by the salt but also by the decaying bodies of animals and man. The people had to drink water from somewhere — either fresh water from wells or contaminated water. We chose to try to offer fresh water for these survivors.

But it was not all that easy. After the process of sinking the well was completed, we pulled out the pipe. Then an approved filter was fastened on the end of the pipe. The pipe was again put down into the small hole which it had made. The little hand pump was fastened to the pipe. We prayed as the pump was primed. The Muslims called out in the "name of Allah." Would the water be fresh or salty. No one knew until it had been tasted.

Everyone nearby tasted the water. Rarely did we find fresh water the first attempt. When we failed, we quickly pulled the pipe out, moved some distance away and began the process all over with that prayer still being uttered.

However when there was fresh water, news went out across the countryside. In a few minutes, people could be seen coming from all directions with their containers. That which I had so often taken for granted, a drink of water, was precious to them. We discovered that some Bengalis walked as far as eight miles to get fresh water.

R. T. and I first began working in Char Bata. We had never heard of the place, but we soon learned the area had been densely populated; now it was different. About fifty percent of the people had died in the tragedy. Ninety-five percent of the houses had been destroyed.

One of the first wells was sunk near the home of Ataur Ali. Mr. Ali lost twenty-one members of his greater family. Along with him a young man and two little girls survived. In the village where their six little houses had stood, the four were living under branches which had been cut from the palm trees.

They did not have to go through the process of funerals. The ocean, ten miles away, became the grave for the members of this family. The four helped us carry the supplies for the well. After the third attempt, we left a well that was producing only a small amount of water. We again had wanted to help but were so helpless ourselves when it came to finding abundant fresh water.

As I walked about between the well sites, I often thought that perhaps I would have "given up" if I had been caught in such circumstances. The few men whom I met on the paths often wanted to talk. Each one wanted to tell of what had happened to him and his family. I wondered, "How will they ever be able to pull themselves together and live even half-way normally?"

One morning when I was moving between well sites, I heard the pitiful cry of a woman. I had been moving quickly to make sure the work was proceeding as fast as possible. This, of course, was not the first time I had heard women wailing in the area. But I felt compelled to stop. I saw her on the little path.

Her voice shrieked as she screamed out to Allah, "I want my baby! I want my baby!" Pain rang out from this troubled soul. Dozens of other mothers in villages nearby were crying out or cramped within not only for this mother but also for hundreds and even thousands who had lost their little ones.

I tried to think of some of the ways it had happened. Some had climbed trees with babies in their arms. The physical strain was too much. They had let their babies slip and then fall down into the devouring water. Most of the babies were never seen again. Others, frightened when the wave thundered into the village area, had their babies plucked from their arms as they stood helplessly in the swirling water. But perhaps even more tragic were the mothers who, when they heard the roar of the wave and then felt the water strike their feet, could not remember where their little ones were lying.

That morning was Sunday morning. It was "church" time. But here I was, squatting on the little path. My clothes has been chosen to blend somewhat with the surroundings. A torn white T-shirt, sandals without socks and the trousers of a laborer were more than sufficient.

Home in Feni was about fifty miles away. The mother of my four children was not crying out in agony as were these mothers. I was as proud as any father could be. And at that moment I was as grateful to God as any man. Betty and my children were gathered at worship with the few Christians in Feni. My children were well; they had never known real tragedy.

I had to say that between God and me everything was going quite well. Then I began walking on toward the next well site. But I walked slowly. It seemed to me that God Himself got down on that slick, slimy path.

What a time of worship, and I had doubted that He even cared about these people, or at least, if so why did this horrible tragedy happen? But now I knew He cared. He cared about these Bengalis, and He cared about my family back in Feni. Though it was Sunday, I had to say, "No more time for worship now, God, but can't You please stay with me? I need You. In fact, I probably need You as much as that lonely forsaken mother crying out in agony. But God, I do say, I will try to make it possible for others to know that You love us all."

Now, can I not say, I heard Him speak, "Long before you, my friend, I have been on this little path, and long after you I will be on this little path? But I am glad I found you here today trying to tell others and to show others that I am here." I was glad I had found Him in that mess. He really helped. He helps. I had lost time, so I began running to the next well site. Water was needed.

Often when my lunch is late, my head begins to ache; but those days were different. Most of the time I loaded, my vehicle with supplies at night and then moved out to the disaster area long before the break of day. My family was always helpful. Betty would call just in time for me to dress before breakfast. I dressed quickly, ate, grabbed my sack lunch and was off for the day and part of the night.

Sometimes when I returned home at night, I carried the sack lunch just as I had taken it that morning. I was not fasting, at least the way I understood fasting. It just seemed that God had taken away some of the desire to eat.

While I was working in Char Bata, not too far from an ocean channel, I asked the people of one village, "How did you escape death?" One of the men replied, "We heard the mighty roar of the wave. Quickly we went outside our little house. The water rose around our feet. Then there was a strong wave. It tore our little house apart. One side of the frame floated, and we were able to climb upon it." He pointed with his finger. "The wave carried us in that direction. The wooden frame struck that coconut tree. We quickly, one by one, climbed the tree." I had no reason to doubt this fantastic story. The tree to which he pointed was southwest of where we were standing. Trees still leaned southwest, the direction of the out-going wave.

A family of seven who lived nearby told their story. "We felt the water touch our feet when we were sitting on the side of the bed. We quickly ran outside and climbed trees." Six of the seven members of the family survived.

Next door, another family was not able to react so quickly; six of the seven members of that family perished. The young man who had survived seemed to have lost all purpose for living.

We often worked with the helicopters of France, West Germany and the United States flying over our heads. They were dropping food in the areas that were inaccessible to trucks and boats. When I heard that the helicopters had suddenly been taken away, I was angry. I thought, "Why couldn't they be left for this country to use at times of tragedy like this?" Four and one-half months later I was glad they had been taken away, for they would have been used by an army to kill.

It always troubled me as to why the government of Pakistan did not send some of its own military helicopters from West Pakistan to help. Though I rarely mentioned it and then only to foreigners, I thought the Pakistan government, headed by General Yahya Khan, did not care about what happened to Bengalis and especially to Bengalis in the low lying coastal areas. But four and one-half months later I also was glad that the Pakistan helicopters had not been sent to East Pakistan. They, too, would have been available for killing.

Resentment against West Pakistan grew deeply during the time we worked in the disaster area. Often, even in remote places where most of the people do not read, huge signs were seen saying,

"Our foreign friends have come to help us; where are our West Pakistani brothers?"

One morning I left home at 3:00 a.m. and at 6:00 a.m. arrived at Char Alexander where my two missionary companions had spent the nights. Carl Ryther was sleeping on a wooden school bench under the open sky since the roofing of the little building we were using as headquarters had been destroyed by the storm which had accompanied the tidal wave.

R. T. had taken the seat out of his Volkswagen microbus and was sleeping on the floor of the bus. After preparing their breakfast, I called them to eat. They ate hurriedly and were off for a day's hard work.

Some time after they departed, the soldiers who had been sleeping in a brick building nearby began to stir. They always seemed to have the best of what was available. Every time I was near their quarters, they appeared to have sufficient time to lounge around. Often I found myself wishing for help from them since the strong, husky soldiers could have easily carried the pumps and other supplies. If they ever did any work, I did not see it. However the newspapers carried pictures and stories of what they were supposedly doing. It was not difficult for me to understand the feeling of the Bengalis against the West Pakistan dominated army.

On November 13th, the main government officer in our district was not in Noakhali, so the second in command Mr. Anisur Rahman, took charge without hesitating. He ordered young government officers out to the remote areas where the tidal wave had apparently struck. His order to them was, "Go and try to establish a headquarters. When we have supplies, we will send them to you."

Three weeks later, two of those young men rode back to the district office with R. T. and me. Mr. Sen, a Hindu who was a Third Class Magistrate, told of wading water early the morning of November 13th. He walked for eighteen miles to his destination. Often the water was up to his neck, but that was not the worst part of it. Again and again his feet struck flesh. He had no way of determining whether it was human or animal.

Working in such circumstances under physical strain is not the usual role of young Bengali government officers. As we were riding out of the disaster area, one of them fell asleep. His head gradually toppled over on the shoulder of one of the tube-well workmen. The workman's clothes were dirty and filled with perspiration to the degree that we had to keep the vehicle thoroughly ventilated. I have wished for a photograph of that scene to help me recall the experience of the elite working or resting with the common man.

Not all Bengalis, however, had the attitude of Mr. Sen and his companion Magistrate. When we first entered the Char Bata area, the gentleman who showed us where we would be working got into our vehicle and adjusted his pistol in the holster. I asked, "What is the purpose of that?" His reply was, "You never know what these savage people will do to you."

A few days later as we went to the actual work site, two armed policemen accompanied us. When the government officer was ready to depart, he said, "I will leave these two policemen with you." My reply was, "What for? If we cannot work in peace without an armed guard, there is no need for us to be here." The policemen left with him.

We did have trouble in that area. One man stole some supplies for a well. But we turned to the people and asked that they recover them. Two days later the man who had taken the supplies brought them back. He had been forced to do so by the local people.

In another area, practically everything had been destroyed. The survivors were fighting for their existence. We had two hundred blankets to distribute among several thousand people. One group felt it was not receiving its share. A big fight broke out. The village leader, the relief officer, and the policemen who were with them fled. I knew we missionaries were not being blamed for the manner of distribution. I also knew that these innocent people would not harm me; so after they pushed and shoved for about an hour, they settled down. We had a long talk and worked out the situation. We needed no policemen or guns.

No one could have done a better job of "sinking tube wells" than R. T. Only a few days following the disaster, he had the ability to joke with the people; and they needed this. He could do it because they were sure of his faithfulness to them.

After three attempts on two consecutive days in one area, Batirtak, R. T. pulled the pipe, brought out all of the supplies, and came by my home in Feni enroute to Comilla. He seemed somewhat dejected. His face did not carry the usual smile. He had walked twelve miles each of those two days and after the six attempts, he had found only salty water. I knew how I felt after such a failure, but it became more real as he spoke few words and moved on toward his home and family for the night.

As he drove away, before entering my house, I wiped away the tears. I believe that R. T. did the same as he drove. We wanted to help, but often it seemed that we were able to do little. But we did not forget the isolated people of Batirtak.

Several days later some of the men from this area came requesting the supplies. "We will do all the work. Just give us the materials," they pleaded. With R. T.'s consent, I gave them the supplies. They excitedly reported that they had found fresh water. I went to examine it. It tasted great. But they had sunk the well in a low area. Mud was everywhere. There was only one way out. We pulled the pipe, moved a short distance away, and on a little ridge put the well down. The eighth attempt and the answer to prayer and determination — beautiful fresh water flowed from the little pump. I called it "A well of water given in the name of Jesus." During the early days of the war, I visited Batirtak with Mr. Alam and other leaders in our district. The fresh water was still flowing.

The longer we worked, the more apparent it became why we had been asked by the government officer to attempt this work. Apparently everyone but us was aware of the difficulty of finding good water in the low coastal areas. But it seemed the real reason we had been asked was that since we were missionaries, God would be good to us and we would find fresh water.

Sometimes after we had attempted to find fresh water several times, the people said, "We had tried many times in past years but now were hoping you might be successful." Though this was irritating to us, we did not blame them for attempting anything.

Occasionally I found myself questioning God. Why did such terrible natural disasters happen in the first place? And why did they have to strike on one of the least developed areas of the world? Why could not we, at least, find a well of water for these who had suffered and were suffering so much? I still do not know those answers.

Often we missionaries became tired. For some of us, the work day began long before the sun had begun to show its face. The work day ended long after most other people were asleep. However I did not hear any complaints about this. I saw in my companions determination, a willingness to do hard labor and to walk miles through the mud in the low lying ocean areas, but never did I hear complaints about weary bodies.

Pastor Halder and Tom Thurman came from Faridpur, many miles away, to give us a boost. They were a good walking team. In one area five wells were needed. I asked them to do two wells about twelve miles away from the last road. They moved out early one morning with a team of workman. Later that day, I left with two teams for an area eight miles away to put down the remaining three wells.

When darkness fell, my three wells were producing good water. The workman said, "We must hurry or the ocean tide water will cut us off for most of the night." We hurried. The first channel of water appeared to have us cut off. The Bengali men said, "Please feel free to take off all your clothes if you like, for you will get very cold with wet clothing." They took the supplies I was carrying. I stripped down as much as my missionary modesty permitted. We waded the water. It struck my chest. A Bengali was on my left and another on my right. They were not sure I could manage in the swift cold tide water. Neither was I sure. But we made it. I put on my dry clothes which one of them had carried on his head. We moved quickly toward the next channel. I felt that I was really beginning to know the people among whom I had lived for more than twelve years.

The next channel was deeper. My fear was greater. The clouds had covered the moon and stars. We struggled through the channel. I was glad it was dark. No one could detect the feeling that my face must have expressed. Three and one-half hours later, we reached the vehicle. My body was tired. I calculated I had walked twenty-four miles — eight miles in and eight out, and roughly eight miles between the three wells. Much of the time I was barefoot in the mud. But what about Tom and Pastor Halder?

I sat down in a little dilapidated hut. The radio was blasting out in Bengali. I had forgotten. Today was election day in all of Pakistan except for the disaster area. The results were being announced. Screams of joy rang out. Sheik Mujibur Rahman and his Awami League was winning almost everything in East Pakistan. It appeared early that he would be Pakistan's first democratically elected president. I was tired but happy — happy because the people around me were happy, but I was also hopeful. I was hopeful that because of this election, the Bengalis of East Pakistan would have a better life.

29

Early that morning I had told Pastor Halder and Tom that I would not wait long for them if I returned before they did, so I drove home.

I awakened early the next morning and drove out to the same area. Tom and Pastor Halder had not returned. I began to think of all that might have happened to them. There was only one thing to do. I walked in what I thought was the direction in which they had gone. There was a high mound of earth in one village area. I sat down hoping that I would see them in the distance. I saw a group of men walking in my direction, but they were too far away to recognize. A few minutes later I could see them clearly. It was Tom, Pastor Halder and the crew of Bengali workmen.

The tide water had cut them off. They had no choice but to sleep out in the cold ocean area. All the houses had been destroyed, but they had slept in a straw stack. Two Bengali workmen had shared a blanket with Tom. The village people had sacrificed to make this available for them. But they reported two wells of fresh water. This was all that counted.

In the early afternoon, I was embarrassed when I had to ask my companions for their permission to go home. I was terribly sick. When I reached home, I had nothing to say to Betty and the children. Seven days a week most of the time for the past month, and long days at that, had been too much for my fragile frame. My body ached. Several hours later I awakened. I felt much better. I was not sick; I was exhausted.

Time came for the evening meal. Betty told me about the visit of an extremely kind and gracious man while I was sleeping. She had offered to awaken me; but when he learned I had come home sick, he asked her to please let me rest. He would come later.

That night Mr. Alam came with a friend. They were two most impressive Bengali gentlemen. They had learned about our tube well work from the district headquarters. The question was, "When this project was completed, then what would we do?" I answered, "We will go again to the government officer in charge of Noakhali." They told of the possibility of a model village being constructed in one of the areas where we had put down wells. They wanted our assistance in this project.

Though I felt closely drawn to Mr. Alam and his companion, Mr. Abdur Rab Chaudhury, I was hesitant to make any commitment. I had about sixty thousand U. S. dollars, which had been given to me by concerned groups outside of our organization, to use in the disaster area. I asked for time to discuss their proposal with Mr. Buckley.

When they left our house that night, I was not aware that I had just talked with the "diplomat turned farmer" and with the Relief Coordinator for Noakhali District and for Chittagong District. Mr. Alam had said Mr. Chaudhury lost twenty-two members of his greater family in the disaster. I later discovered that no two Bengalis in all of East Pakistan commanded so much of my respect. They seemed to permeate honesty and dedication to hard work.

The government officer sent us to distribute blankets in Char Alexander. This was fast, easy work compared to sinking tube wells. It also meant fast use of money and probably was not nearly so necessary as other work we could have done. It was completed in a short time. I was glad, for there was no way to tell who should receive the blankets. During the last few days of blanket distribution, we met Mr. Alam in Char Alexander.

It was raining that morning. Men whose houses had been destroyed and parts of their land washed out into the huge river channel near the ocean, had come to Mr. Alam with the plea to do something about the model village immediately. R. T. and I were their hope. We consented to provide the metal roofing for the houses and to give our moral support to the project. The next day we stood by the side of Mr. Alam and other Muslim men and offered a prayer to God asking for his blessings on the first model village in East Pakistan.

Regardless of how much I may have felt drawn to the people of Noakhali, we had to leave Feni. There was no value in a temporary place. If we were going to remain in the country with four children, then we would have to find a place to settle down that was agreeable, at least, to Cherie and Kathy. So we left Feni, our home in Noakhali District.

CHAPTER THREE

Cherie and Kathy, though fearful of what might happen, were reasonable with me concerning our departing Feni. We as a family had taken another of our missionary families, the James Youngs, to visit Char Bata the day before Christmas, 1970. That visit had left a deep impression upon my little girls. They, their mother, and Mrs. Young talked with Muslim women in the village. Because of Muslim social customs, I had not talked with village women.

The stories they heard that day were startling. In one village the ladies said, "We tried to save the eldest grandmother. When we heard the roar of the wave, we helped her up into a tree. But we never even saw her body again. The wave of water broke the tree in whose branches she was clinging." The ocean had become the grandmother's grave. Cherie and Kathy loved their two grandmothers back in America.

Then, too, they had smelled the stench of death many times when we had washed the rice straw off the vehicle in our driveway. Though I did not tell them much of what had happened, they knew our neighbors had suffered greatly. The local newspaper had carried unbelievable stories, but pictures of destroyed buildings and torn swollen bodies had made them believable.

Cherie and Kathy were patient also because they knew I loved the work in which I was involved. In our district there were hundreds of thousands who had never heard the Gospel. They knew Daddy would have difficulty leaving his responsibility.

It seemed there was no other choice but to leave. By April 12, most of our Bengali friends had left Feni for either India or the village areas of Noakhali.

On April 12th, a young Bengali Muslim came from Comilla.

33

He reported, "I watched the Buckleys' house for several days. But I never did get an opportunity to talk with them. In fact, I never even saw them. But I heard from a friend that they were able to leave Comilla in a military plane for Dacca."

The Buckleys had gone to Dacca. I could no longer do any relief work. Our Bible centers were closed. Feni was left, as best we knew, with one family — my family. I, to be even half-way fair to Betty and the children, had to say "Finish your school examinations, and we will leave."

I deny that paternalism or spiritual colonialism kept me in Feni. It was our home. I belonged there as best I could understand. This was God's mission for me and my family.

Six and one-half years earlier, we had arrived in Feni to prepare the way for building a hospital. Forty-five years before our arrival, the Australian Baptists, due to a lack of personnel, had left this area. When we first arrived, Mr. Watson, an elderly retired Australian Missionary who had lived in Comilla, wrote me a challenging letter concerning the opportunities for Christ in Noakhali.

Two American Peace Corps young men had been in Feni when we arrived. They left, never to return, during the 1965 India-Pakistan war. At the Canadian Catholic Mission, thirty miles from Feni, there were no foreign children. So, for approximately fifty years, until our arrival in 1965, no foreign family had lived in Noakhali among her estimated three million people. Now we prepared to leave, perhaps never to return. If we crossed the border into India as refugees and the West Pakistanis continued to dominate the Bengalis of East Pakistan, we believed we would not be permitted to return. We did not have visas for Pakistan. We were only permitted to remain until time for our next furlough.

The Charles Becketts of our mission, who had lived in Feni before time for their furlough, had been refused permission to return to Pakistan.

But leave, we must. We had first arrived in Feni thinking a hospital would be built. This effort had been a failure. The governor of East Pakistan at that time, Monem Khan, had only one excuse for not giving permission for the hospital. "You are planning to use too much of our valuable land," he had said. This had seemed a rather weak reason. The official reply came four years after our application was first made, "We are sorry to inform you that permission for your hospital is denied." Except for a few leading politicians in the governor's party, the people of Feni had supported us in the request. That was now only history for us.

The late afternoon of April 14th I talked with a relative of my deceased friend, the cycle rickshaw operator, Dhanu Mia. He agreed to have six cycle rickshaws at our house by daybreak the next morning.

We wanted to reach Dacca if at all possible. Other missionaries would be there. We could discuss plans with them. But Dacca was one hundred miles away. The question was how could we get there?

My mind was torn with three alternatives. We could travel west through Noakhali District for fifty miles. But that would only leave us in a remote area without roads. The fact that village people would help us through the district made it appealing, however. We could travel northwest toward Laksam on village paths. But this would all be unknown territory for me. The best route, however, seemed to be the highway we had always traveled when going to Dacca. We knew our vehicle could not go more than four miles because of destroyed bridges. However, since this route followed closely the Indian border, we might encounter Pakistani soldiers and Freedom Fighters in battle. But even so, we could cross the border into India as refugees.

I really wasn't rational enough to determine what appeared to be the best route. Leaving home under such circumstances was not an easy thought for me. Surely, we prayed, and it wasn't routine stuff. We needed help, but often it seemed that we could not understand the answer.

Betty and the children packed four suitcases. They crammed school books into handbags. We pulled carrots and celery from our garden. A few boxes of cookies completed our food supply. Just before we went to bed, I told Betty, "I believe we should follow the regular route and hope for the best." The alarm awakened us early the next morning.

The six cycle rickshaws came ahead of schedule. The previous afternoon we took the tires off our Volkswagen microbus and removed the batteries from the bus and a pick-up truck we had used for relief work. We expected the army to try to use them; so if possible, we were going to prevent that. We discovered that putting everything we wanted to save into four suitcases was not easy. It was especially difficult for Cherie and Kathy. They kept saying, "Mother, but can't we take this?" Neither was it easy for Betty to refuse their requests so many times.

I had tried to get some men to travel with us. Sultan, who had worked for us since we first arrived in Feni, said the night before, "I will travel with you. You will need me to help you." Also two of the Christian young men with whom we worked promised they would go. That morning only Daniel, one of the Christians, was ready. It was apparent they were afraid of the army we might encounter on the road. However I had no right to blame them for this.

At 6:00 a.m., April 15th, we climbed into the cycle rickshaws. That climb was difficult. I told Betty and the children, "We will probably never see this home again."

It is ordinarily blazing hot in Bangladesh in April. But that morning we wore sweaters. A cool breeze fanned our faces as the rickshaws rolled outside the gate. That breeze helped dry the tears. The rickshaws took a bypass through village areas, so we missed the main part of town.

We had carefully divided the luggage. Keith rode with me in front. Cherie and Kathy were next in line, each with a rickshaw. The fourth rickshaw was empty except for some luggage. We took it because of the possibility of a breakdown of one of the others. Betty and Wade rode together. Daniel was in the last rickshaw.

The riding seat of a cycle rickshaw sits on hard springs over two wheels which are about three feet apart. There is space for one's feet and a small amount of luggage just in front of the seat. The seat is tilted forward to help the rickshaw move more easily. Because of this, the sitting position is somewhat uncomfortable.

There is a canopy over the seat to protect the passenger from the sun and rain. As the canopy strikes the wind, it hinders the speed; so we kept it folded back. The front part of the rickshaw is just like the front part of a bicycle including the driver's seat. As we started, the rickshaw operator's bare feet moved the pedals with lightning speed.

I immediately began watching the mileage markers on the road. It was forty miles to Comilla. We had allotted two days for that part of the journey. During the first hour's travel only one bridge had been destroyed. I told Betty and the children, "It seems impossible. We have covered seven miles in an hour."

But the rickshaw drivers were using nervous energy. Though the sun was covered by clouds and the air was cool, they soon became wet with perspiration. I suggested that they take a rest. They refused. I soon understood. They wanted to take us as far as they thought was reasonably safe, then quickly return to their families near Feni. They feared meeting the army.

I talked with them as we rode. They spoke of Dhanu Mia, their friend and mine, who had been killed by the planes. I chose to believe they were not taking us on this dangerous journey for money. They were taking us because of my sorrow and shock at the way our common friend had been killed. It was their way of thanking me.

Several times they asked, "Sir, what will the army do to us?" I could only answer, "I do not know, but you flee to a remote area when you know the army is coming." One of them asked, "Will you return to Feni some day?" The answer did not come out easily. "We will, if it is possible," I uttered. The "if" was not pleasing to them or to me.

During the second, third and fourth hours, the road became almost impassable. Bridge after bridge had been destroyed by the Bengalis to stop that angry killing army. Sometimes we had extreme difficulty in getting the rickshaws down over the debris and up again. The thing that saved us was the number of drivers, for all the drivers converged on one rickshaw at a time and lifted it over the obstruction. Ditches had been cut across the road. That would stop an army but delayed us only momentarily.

The village people had placed many trees across the road. A beautiful thing happened at some of these points. I had told the children, "Always quickly jump down with your hand luggage when we reach an obstruction." Betty naturally, with Wade had to get down more slowly. On a few occasions before she got down, village men standing nearby grabbed her rickshaw and lifted it over the fallen trees. We moved on quickly. Every act of kindness like this made us wish we could be back in Feni.

We met Freedom Fighters from Feni up to fifteen miles north. They were there to meet the army before it reached their families in the villages. I visualized their young flesh torn to bits by the army's automatic weapons.

At the end of the fourth hour, we approached the largest market place between Feni and Comilla. This was almost half the distance to Comilla. I thought, "We may even reach Comilla today." But I did not dare express this optimism to the children. It might be premature. The children were noble. No complaints had been uttered. Before leaving Feni, they agreed to sleep willingly under trees, in a village hut, or any place that was necessary. However I wanted to spare them this.

The rickshaws stopped a short distance from the market place. The leader spoke softly, "We want to turn back. I see Pakistan flags flying ahead of us." While they lighted and smoked homemade cigarettes, we unloaded the rickshaws.

I thanked them with words, paid them well with money and then said, "We hope we will see you again some day." Those were not hollow words. I meant it.

According to their custom, the six Muslim drivers gave us a salute and said "Salaam." This meant, "Peace to you." Then they shook our hands gently. After briefly speaking with local people who had gathered, they jumped on their empty rickshaws. Those bare feet hit the pedals firmly. They moved rapidly. In a few minutes, they were out of sight. We wished the best for them.

Our friends from Feni had "gone beyond their duty." The border of India was a few hundred yards from where we stood. There were no rickshaws in sight. We heard from those who had gathered around us, "The army is not in the market place. The Pakistan Flags were put up today. We hope the army will notice the flags and not burn the market when they arrive." They expected the army at any moment.

"Daddy, what are we going to do?" the children asked. Though they had been good, I had never been more frustrated. I felt like screaming to them, "I don't know!" but I answered calmly, "We will decide soon." Words were few as we waited.

We had traveled this route dozens of times in comfort during the past six and one-half years. But today, how different it was!

Then I recalled that in 1969 we had started to Dacca. We drove seventy miles and had to turn back after learning that the city was under military curfew. There was a rebellion all over Pakistan against the president, Field Marshal Ayub Khan. A few miles north of where we were standing that day, a mob had stopped us. We were not flying a black flag indicating our dissatisfaction with the Field Marshal's government.

The mob knew we were foreigners. There was no need to explain this. The real problem was — they took us to be part of the "establishment." They threatened to burn the microbus with us inside. They argued among themselves. I reved the engine loudly. Those standing in front momentarily jumped to the side. I gunned the accelerator to the floor. We moved quickly toward home. Nine year old Kathy crawled out from under the middle seat of the vehicle. But she was not the only one who had been afraid.

But this day, the number of village people grew quickly. Soon six rickshaws came out of hiding near-by. "We will take you as far as possible," they bravely announced. We did not have to become refugees in India. That day, no one considered us part of the "establishment." We were as desperate as our Bengali friends, maybe even more so.

We moved rapidly toward Comilla. But only about a mile beyond the market it seemed that our journey toward Dacca had again ended. Somewhere a fierce battle was raging. We felt the earth tremble through the soft rickshaw tires. The shells falling some distance away were not small ones. Expressionless, my rickshaw driver looked at me. Then one of the children said, "Oh, Daddy, what will we do?" I replied, "Let's keep moving slowly. Maybe we will be able to understand better what's happening."

The rickshaw drivers concluded that a battle was taking place at Laksam several miles west of us. Undoubtedly, God was in this journey. The night before, one of the alternate routes discussed was through Laksam. After about thirty minutes, the sounds passing off to the left began fading. While others were dying or facing a cruel army, we moved on toward Comilla.

We stopped for rest under a tree. We ate some of our raw carrots, our celery, and our cookies. But we didn't delay long.

Another bridge had been blown out about six miles from Comilla. There had been a thunderstorm in the hills of India nearby. The stream was filled with gushing water. A temporary crossing had been arranged. Banana tree stalks had been tied together. A man was on each side of the stream holding a rope fastened to the stalks. We crossed with our luggage two at a time.

On the other side several rickshaws were waiting. They were ready to travel to Comilla. We watched carefully to see if there were movements as we entered the outskirts of the town. From the reports we had heard, anyone breaking curfew was shot on sight. But the rickshaw drivers would not make that mistake.

As we approached Comilla, I silently reminisced about the joys of the previous years we had spent there. Following a year of language study in Dacca upon our arrival in East Pakistan in 1959, we had moved to Comilla. During the three years there, it was the Comilla Christians who struggled with us as we tried to learn the

39

Bengali language and culture. Now we were "old" missionaries, but the joy of those early days were still real.

But this was certainly not the Comilla we had known. As we entered, the streets were vacant. We heard trucks coming. This was our first view of the army. The trucks were filled with soldiers with rifles pointing in all directions. They had no way of knowing who the "enemy" was. They hardly seemed to notice us. Since we knew the Buckleys were in Dacca, we rode directly to the Catholic school. No one was there.

We decided to ride to the Buckleys' house. Enroute, we met Father Dan, an American and the local Catholic priest, whom we had known for many years. He seemed to be as glad to see us as we were to see him. "Yes, the Buckleys have gone to Dacca," Father Dan said. "Also," he reported, "one of the sisters had fallen from a rickshaw and broken her arm, so the military agreed for all the foreigners to fly to Dacca." He had remained alone.

Father Dan had seen some of the Baptists, but he did not know the circumstances of every one. We rode on to the Buckleys' house.

The rickshaws pulled into the Buckleys' yard. Beautiful screams were heard from the Roys' house next door. "The McKinleys are here!" rang out. "But how did you get here? Are all of you okay?" "Yes, we are all okay, but it will be hard to believe how we got here," I said.

Soon the loud joy settled down. We remembered where we were. Mrs. Roy said, "Come to our house. We will fix tea and cookies. There is nothing to eat in the Buckleys' house." We quietly rejoiced with them and they with us. Then more solemnly we discussed the terrible events of the past few days.

Several Christian families had gone into India, but most of the faithful church members were still in their homes debating what to do. "What do you think, Mr. McKinley, what should we do?" I answered, "I have no advice, but I will help in any other way I can."

The Poddar family had been taken away in an army truck. They had been lined up and threatened with rifles. However, for some unknown reason, they were returned to their home. Some of the Christians thought they had been released because they were related to an American Christian Mission. Pakistan, no doubt, counted on American government support. It was later learned

40

that one of the Poddars' sons was a Freedom Fighter. If the army had known this, the Poddars would probably not have been alive.

The Christians still feared for their lives. They told of some difficulties the Buckleys had to endure. Several young Bengali men were shot to death just outside their gate. There had been one three-day curfew. R. T. had been caught outside during a round of firing. He lay in a ditch until he was able to slip into the house. The army officers refused to believe Fran Buckley had hepatitis. It was the Catholic sister's broken arm that got them out.

R. T. told me a year later that the plane on which they rode to Dacca had only six seats for the two Danes, two American sisters, Fran, Amye, their little three year old daughter, and him. He said, "Our anger boiled because the plane was loaded with a case of bullets marked with a USA stamp." But Amye helped. As the plane took off she asked, "Aren't they even going to be nice enough to serve us candy so our ears won't pop?"

We talked for a long time. Then after a brief rest, we had a good meal of curry and rice with the Roys. But it was not easy to eat their good food, for we wondered when their supply might end.

The town, whose population had been about 100,000, was without electricity and water. There was a well near the Buckleys' house, and I pumped enough water for us to wash before we prepared for sleep.

Everything was quiet. It seemed that not a person was moving. Perhaps no one was. In the stillness of the night, I lay on my back. Wade, who slept with me, soon fell asleep. April 15th had become history, and to me and my family — important history. According to expectations the previous night, we should have been sleeping in a village, under a tree, or under a bridge.

God had managed for us. We had lifted the rickshaws over nineteen destroyed bridges and culverts that day. The ditches and trees across the road had been too many to remember. The frustration, after our Feni friends had turned back, had been troublesome. The fear of meeting the angry army in the country had been real. But now, though some fear remained, there was more assurance that God was managing.

We awakened early the next morning. One of the Christian boys reported, "A bus will depart soon going toward Dacca." Betty found a little rice and some salt in the Buckleys' house. We took those to Mrs. Roy. The Roys had prepared a good breakfast for us.

41

We were being like the new missionaries we had been in 1959. They did everything possible to help us.

Just before we departed in rickshaws for the bus stand, Mrs. Roy said, "When the war is over, we want you and all of the missionaries to come back." The night before I had expressed that possibly after reaching Dacca, Betty and the children would leave for America. But I had also said, "Most likely I will be coming back in a few days." Perhaps Mrs. Roy and the others had not taken my word about my remaining seriously.

After she had spoken, I dared not open my mouth for even one word. Tears would have flooded my face. I knew I would be coming back to Comilla. It was not a place for any family, but these friends had nowhere to go. Her statement had been so honest. We were not being blamed for leaving. We were wanted back even before we left.

As we rode away, I thought, "How can we ever leave people like this?" It seemed to me the deeper the trouble, the greater the danger, the more expression of the real self. In Mrs. Roy, the real self was full of faith.

We boarded the small bus and took seats in front. Passengers began filling the remaining seats. Each tried to make room for others. There was not the usual pushing and shoving for places.

Just before the bus pulled out, one of the Muslim men who had worked with R. T. in sinking tube wells saw us. He came quickly to the bus. "Are all of you okay?" he said. We talked briefly. He departed and returned within a few minutes with a bunch of small knotty bananas. It may have taken more than a half-day's wages to pay for those few bananas — and he was unemployed. As the bus pulled out, I thought, "How can so many people be so kind?"

The bus created excitement. We were on the first bus since March 25th. The Comilla army base was four miles east of town. The bus stopped for a complete search by soldiers. Everyone was tense. The soldiers climbed to the top of the bus where all luggage was stored. One soldier called out, "Where is the key to this metal locker?" No one answered. I did not want the children to experience added fear. I quickly climbed out through the window to the top of the bus. The soldier said, "No, it is not yours. We will not open yours. Only these people are bad." I climbed back into the bus and asked to whom the locker belonged. One man pointed and quietly said, "The lady sitting near the front." Her entire body was covered with a black garment indicating she was a strict Muslim. This meant I should not speak to her, but I did. I said, "Please give me your key, and I will watch as they open it. I will not let them take anything." This was some promise when several soldiers were armed with automatic weapons. I watched as they carefully examined her locker. Soon we moved slowly on.

The children asked, "Daddy, why have so many houses been burned?" Some of the Bengalis indicated that we should not even pretend to see anything. However, we were all soon talking about this man-made tragedy. It was apparent that the army had no friends on our bus.

Twenty miles from Comilla, our bus journey ended. A large bridge had been destroyed. We picked up our luggage and with some help, walked to the other side of the water on an old foot-bridge. We were told, "Wait here; a bus will be coming, and you can go to Dacca on it." I did not believe it. We arranged for some rickshaws and rode twenty miles to the first of many rivers we had to cross in order to reach Dacca.

Just before we reached the first river, we met a bus that appeared to be a Dacca bus. When we reached the river, our rickshaws were motioned to enter a large ferry. Again we could not believe it. It was a Dacca ferry; and though it would follow the river a long distance, it would eventually take us within twelve miles of Dacca. The ferry was empty except for a few passengers. About an hour later the Dacca bus returned and boarded the ferry. This ferry was part of the army's program to make everything appear normal. "If everything were normal," we thought as we rode, "why are villages near the river going up in smoke and flames?" Though the ferry was physically comfortable, mental anguish tore at us. We sailed safely for about three hours while others died.

Before the ferry docked, I never thought of asking the bus driver if he could take us on to Dacca. Perhaps I thought there was other public transportation. When the ferry docked, the bus pulled off. Some helpers carried our heavy luggage. We climbed down.

I may have been helpless to do anything about it, but I tried. Soldiers teased Betty, Cherie and Kathy. They knew neither Bengali nor English. But my few words only brought laughter. These soldiers, "friends of our home country," were unloading boxes of what I am sure were military supplies. Those boxes had the markings of the United States Government.

We struggled along with our luggage for a short distance. Someone suggested, "Why don't you ask the army officer to arrange transportation?" We were angry enough to have crawled rather than to have asked this army for transportation. They were killing our friends and our neighbors.

Two men approached us. Speaking in Bengali they said, "We will take you to Dacca if you pay us enough." It did not take us long to agree on an amount. As we drove along, I wondered, "Why do they drive on this road for any amount?" Buildings had been blasted with shells from tanks, with rockets from planes and with bombs. The smaller houses along the entire route had been burned.

The two drivers kept speaking without pointing, "Look to the left," or "look to the right." They tried to fill our eyes with the destruction. They succeeded. Taxis, like the ones in which we rode, were charred metal. The usually crowded highway was desolate.

We reached the eastern side of Dacca and became quite excited. We discussed, "What will we say to the missionaries at the Guest House?" There was much to talk about. We drove through the city. It was as if we owned it. There were no obstructions. The city seemed more desolate than the road.

The buses blasting their horns, the trucks moving at a dangerous speed, the cycle rickshaws, the push carts, the cumbersome cowdrawn carts, the few private cars, the mini taxis, and the thousands of pedestrians had left the streets of Dacca. A few men peeped around the corners of buildings from the alleys. Since a man's life had become so cheap, the masses were in hiding. The store doors were bolted and locked. Except for military vehicles, our two taxis were the only vehicles seen on the journey of twelve miles to our mission's Guest House.

The Guest House door was locked. A note told us where the key was. Our spirits, so excited at first, dipped to a very low point.

CHAPTER FOUR

The locked doors of the Guest House stared us coldly in the face. A note hanging on the door said, "If you want to use the Guest House, please come to me for the key." It was signed, "Phil Parshall." Phil was with another missionary organization and a friend of ours.

I paid the taxi drivers and began searching for a cycle rickshaw that would take me to the Parshalls. As I rode, I thought, "What will our children do? They counted so much on seeing the other missionary children."

At the sound of Phil's doorbell, "Jim McKinley," rang out, "where did you come from? How are Betty and the children?" He kept talking. "We tried every known way to get some news concerning you. You are the answer to the prayer of every Christian in Dacca."

We were joined by Edd Welch, Phil's missionary companion. As we sat down, I asked, "What about our missionaries?" Phil answered, "Four of your families went to West Pakistan and may be going to the States."

"What about other foreign families?" I asked. "As far as we know, there are no foreign wives or children in the city. Even many of the Catholic sisters are gone," was his reply.

"What will my children do?" I thought. "Can they ever be happy in a situation like this?"

Phil went on to explain, "The Rythers of your mission went to Faridpur and are living with the Tom Thurmans, I understand. My family, as well as Edd's left for West Pakistan." He then asked, "What are you going to do?" I replied, "It's impossible to say now. We will have to wait and see how Cherie and Kathy feel."

Phil gave me the Guest House key as we walked to the door. "I'll come over tomorrow and give you the safe keys, the money I have which belongs to your mission and some financial records." I thanked Phil for helping us and quickly climbed into the cycle rickshaw which had waited for me.

Poor Dacca had really taken a beating. The streets were so quiet they seemed ready to explode. Even the ringing of the rickshaw bell caused people to look out over the brick walls in the residential area of Dhanmondi.

I was soon "home" at the mission Guest House. Betty and the children were still sitting on the luggage. "Did you get the key?" Betty asked. "Yes, I have it." Cherie then put forth the inevitable question, "Daddy, where are our missionaries?" There was no choice but to answer, "Four families have gone. The Rythers and Thurmans are in Faridpur," I replied.

This struck Cherie and Kathy rather severely. Cherie asked, "But, Daddy, how can we live by ourselves with all that is happening?" I could only answer, "Cherie, I don't know, but let's try to be patient and wait and see."

Kathy usually does most of the talking so she joined the questioning, "Why did the others leave?" I answered, "Kathy, we have seen enough since we left the ferry about two hours ago to make anyone leave this city. They all must have endured the deepest fear. They probably even thought we had crossed the border into India."

We were joined by two Bengali Guest House employees and then went inside. The Guest House was downstairs. The Truman Moores had lived upstairs. The soft chairs in the Guest House living room were welcomed.

As darkness approached, I told Betty and the children, "Trying to do my duty as missionary chairman, I wrote a letter to all of our missionary families about six weeks ago. I told them that if the political situation worsened, each family should decide for itself what it should do. I also said that we all should support one another regardless of the decisions made."

This "report" to my family moved us beyond another barrier. They accepted, I thought, very well the decisions made by our missionary companions. They knew that "Aunt" Fran Buckley was sick with hepatitis. We all learned later that "Uncle" James Young was desperately sick in West Pakistan with the same trouble. He was not sure, regardless of the political situation, that he would ever be able to return to Bangladesh.

The Truman Moores had planned to go home on regular furlough in June. It was only natural that they should leave. Then, too, their four children attended the American school in Dacca. It no longer existed. The Don Joneses were transferring to Taiwan so they decided to leave. Two of their sons were also in boarding school in West Pakistan, and they had been cut off from them.

Though my family seemed to accept our situation, when I began trying to pull things together, especially the finances of our mission, I found myself blaming the men for leaving. However, down deep, I knew they had every right to go.

There was no doubt about how we would sleep. It was only deciding in which room. For more than a month, the six of us had slept in the same room. Night time deepened our fears, for the stories we soon heard were frightening, indeed.

Soldiers were entering houses as they desired. Sometimes the family members went unharmed. Often, however, the young women were taken away. In July, a reporter for an international magazine told us that more than five hundred young Bengali women were being kept on the army base at Dacca. I questioned his source of information and said, "Surely, you do not have enough facts to publish this?" He cursed and said, "Yes, I will publish it!"

He explained his source. A Bengali doctor had been asked by the army to go to the base to abort babies of those young Bengalis being kept for use by the soldiers. The doctor had refused to go and had given him the information.

We carefully locked the doors at night and pushed furniture against them, never knowing what might happen before the light of another day. Our only weapon was our limited faith in God.

The stories continued to grow, and most of the time I believed them. This hatred of the West Pakistani soldiers against the Bengalis was evident. One theory was that since all of the Bengalis could not be killed, a new breed of people could be raised. So the soldiers freely used the young women.

During our first few weeks in Dacca, Betty, Cherie, and Kathy stayed inside the house if it were possible. We did not want to draw attention to ourselves. Eventually we began to feel that foreigners were relatively safe.

After our first night in Dacca, we seemed to gather badly

47

needed courage. I informed Rev. Wenger at the British Baptist Mission that we had arrived in Dacca. Also I reported our presence to the American Consulate by phone. Good things continued to happen. I called Mark Tucker, a Southern Baptist with the Cholera Research Laboratory. Mark said, "I will see you tomorrow."

The American Consul General asked me if I would please come to his office for a debriefing. This seemed to be the proper thing to do, so I gladly consented. Phil Parshall went to the Consulate with me. I was surprised when Mr. Blood, the Consul General, took us into a large office filled with important looking people. He introduced us to all of them.

My family's arrival in Dacca seemed of great interest to them. We had traveled one hundred miles. We had come from a border area. We had lived with Bengalis who were fighting for freedom, and no harm had come to us. We had come from an area still controlled by Bengali Freedom Fighters.

Among those present in that office were an American Army Colonel and a British Major, both dressed in civilian clothing. I did not understand their presence and naturally guarded my remarks. I noticed one well dressed gentleman primarily because he did not seem interested in what was being said. Though I do not recall his name, I understood that he was the Deputy Chief of the American Embassy and had come over from West Pakistan to study the situation in East Pakistan.

When I accepted the invitation to this meeting, I felt the Consul General was sympathetic to the Bengali freedom struggle, or otherwise I would have refused. The questions first centered around how we had been able to live in such a situation, especially since we were so near the border of India. The full details of our journey were also sought.

Then we talked about the fighting in the Feni area. I described the circumstances as best I could. We then came to what seemed to be the reason for my presence there. "Are the Bengalis armed?" someone asked. I answered freely what I knew. "Do you think the Bengalis can hold the Feni area?" another one asked. "No, I do not think so," I replied. "The Bengalis are up against a well trained, well equipped army, and they have only meager arms," I said. "With their planes, the West Pakistani forces can drive the Freedom Fighters into India or kill all of them," I admitted sorrowfully.

Then I did what I had determined I would not do. I became deeply emotional. "When my wife and my children were lying in

48

the hallway of our house, I knew the planes zooming over us were planes made in my country. They were killing my friends and my neighbors," I said with wet eyes.

Then suddenly the nicely dressed American gentleman from West Pakistan burst out, "You cannot prove the planes were supplied by America!" I loudly answered, "I can do as well proving it as you can of disproving it!" The exchange grew hotter. But I could not lose. In the 1965 India-Pakistan war, I had read several sources stating that the Sabre 86 planes of the Pakistan Air Force were supplied by America. My "foe" tried to establish that the planes had been provided by Canada. I accepted this as a political lie. It may have been a bantam-weight against a heavy-weight, but America was as much my country as his. I loved her and did not want my country to be involved in killing innocent people. Neither did I want my country to give arms to suppress a freedom struggle against a ruthless military dictatorship.

It had been reported that one plane had been shot down in the Feni area. I was asked about this, "Yes, I heard this in Feni but cannot substantiate it," I answered. "But I do know that after the planes struck Feni the second time, I inquired if there were machine guns available. I felt these could be placed in several of the higher buildings; and since the planes came in so low, perhaps they could be shot down."

With this statement, there was movement in the room. Perhaps they expected me to say I had been involved in fighting after hearing my feelings expressed about the brutality of the West Pakistanis against the Bengalis.

"However," I remarked further, "no such weapons are available." Then I said, "I do not even know if with light weapons a plane could be shot down." One of the military personnel answered, "It is possible." Though I was sorry I had expressed my deepest feeling so openly, I felt encouraged. The Bengalis would surely get help from someone. They would not have to continue as servants.

Most of those present shook my hand and thanked me for coming. The Consul General said, "I don't suppose you want me to provide transportation for you and your family out of the country, do you?" He posed the question properly; but I answered, "No thanks, Sir. Dacca, for us, is a haven of rest compared to where we have been and everything we have seen."

Then he asked, "But what about your food supply? Can I help you?" I replied, "No thanks. We will manage." He was kind, but at that moment, I didn't want anything from the government of my country.

As Phil and I started out the door, Mr. Blood called out, "Wait, we want to help you send messages to your families in America." I hesitated, then went into another room with one of his assistants.

I was determined to use as little U. S. Government money as possible, so I wrote the code address of our Foreign Mission Board, "AMBAPTIST RICHMOND USA." Then I wrote "ARRIVED DACCA SAFELY." I knew Dr. J. D. Hughey, our Area Secretary, would call Betty's mother and my parents immediately.

But Mr. Blood's assistant handed me another piece of paper and said, "Please write out the full address and give more information for your two families. This is not right." I think he knew how I felt. I gave in and wrote a longer message to Dr. Hughey.

As Phil and I departed, I thought, "Governments can be so cruel and ruthless; and yet many government personnel are so human, so kind. Why can't governments then be more decent in their behavior?"

I felt bad as we left the building. But Phil said, "Jim, I was proud of you. It may not have helped, but you gave the Deputy Chief the right answer." Phil's words helped me, but I doubt that there was anything any American citizen could have done to influence the position of his government. I did not believe our government was interested in humanity. It was interested only in what might most benefit its position among the nations of the world.

My conscience troubled me, for in Feni I had really thought of killing in order to stop the killing. On the other hand, I am sure that I would not have had the courage to man a machine gun. I would like to believe that had the opportunity come, my faith would not have permitted me to attempt it. I received help from Rev. Wenger, British Baptist missionary friend, who had been a chaplain in the British army. He said, "Your feelings are perfectly natural. You saw your friends and neighbors being killed. You wanted to stop the killing."

On Sunday morning we gathered with a small group of Christians, all foreigners, at the Holy Family Hospital, a Red Cross institution, for worship. Mr. Wenger, our British friend, was pastor of the International Christian Church. Mark Tucker was also present. This Southern Baptist "connection" was helpful to us because Mark was "Uncle" Mark to our children. His family had been evacuated in early April.

Mark showed us several areas of Dacca city. We saw where many Bengali policemen had been slaughtered the night of March 25th. There was nothing but ashes left of their barracks. The tanks had fired shells into the concrete office buildings. Chips of concrete had been blasted out as thousands of bullets had wildly pierced them.

We drove to the old section of the city. One vast area of wood and hardware stores was left in ashes. The sight of that fire had driven the Bengalis into the deepest fear.

All of the open market places had been left in ashes, as had almost all of the bustees where the city sweepers and other poor people had lived. These poor people had openly supported Sheik Mujibur Rahman in the election. But now, Sheik Mujibur was reportedly in a West Pakistan prison. Though he had won the democratic election, the army was branding him as a traitor. They were attempting to kill all of his supporters. This was some task, but it seemed they were being rather successful.

Mark took us out to lunch. On the way home as we drove past one bustee three blocks from the Guest House, he said, "I wonder why they left this one?" That night we smelled smoke. We heard rifle firing. The next day only ashes were left in that bustee area.

Dacca was fast becoming a "clean" city, and the newspapers were again being published. We read, "The government is cleaning out the slum areas and will replace them with modern markets." Within a month's time the army began proclaiming, "All is back to normal in East Pakistan." This was a big boast, for we learned later that Feni held out against the army until April 24th. Other areas were still under Bengali control. These areas included sections of our Noakhali District that were never taken by the Pakistan army. I was proud we could still consider ourselves as "citizens" of Noakhali.

Betty, Cherie and Kathy began to walk about in the yard, and as we expected, everyone soon knew there was a foreign family in Dacca. This became a magnet. People whom we had never seen before came to the Guest House. Most of them came to express themselves to someone they could trust. I often thought, "If we do nothing but sit and listen, this is reason enough for our remaining here."

51

Some of the men seemed to vent their feelings only through cursing the army. I knew there were other ways. I did not see a place for cursing, but they did not know these ways.

Often strangers asked, "Why do you remain here with your family? It is dangerous." My answer was, "We believe God brought us to this land. We believe He wants us to remain." This was usually the extent of our verbal witness for Christ.

As if enough had not already taken place, we really received a jolt the last of April. A cable came to the Dacca American Consulate from the American Embassy in West Pakistan. It read, "Ryther's daughter emotionally ill." Carla Ryther was in boarding school in Murree, West Pakistan. We still assumed her parents were with our other missionary family, the Tom Thurmans, in Faridpur. Faridpur was a day's journey or about one hundred miles from Dacca.

The cable arrived late that afternoon. We had to get the information to the Rythers. There was only one way to do this. Someone had to take the message. It was too risky to ask a Bengali to make the trip alone. If I went, my family would be alone for at least one night or maybe two nights.

After talking with Betty and the children, Cherie said, "Daddy, you will have to go." That helped. My children loved Carla. If she needed her parents, they were willing for me to attempt the journey, even if it were dangerous.

But I was determined not to leave them alone. I went to see Phil Parshall and Ed Welch. I asked, "Will one of you please stay with my family until I return from Faridpur?" Phil replied, "Ed, if you will stay with Betty and the children, I will go with Jim." That was too much. I objected to his going. "If there is trouble," I said, "it's better if only one person be involved."

The last word was theirs. Ed stayed with my family. Phil and I left at the break of day the next morning. After driving fifty miles, we reached the place where ordinarily one boarded a ferry and traveled from two to four hours depending upon the current. But, of course, there was no ferry. We put the vehicle in a place which we thought was reasonably safe.

Then we hired a small boat and sailed down the Ganges River. After about three hours, we started up a small channel toward the ferry dock. Our boatman suddenly said, "I will have to turn back here." The army was in control of the dock, so the boatman stopped about three miles away. He knew what the army had done and was doing. So we started walking.

Phil and I walked along the river bank. Open trenches seemed untouched. Before long we saw dogs chewing on human flesh at the channel's edge. There had been a battle for the river channel and dock. The bodies had been left for the dogs and buzzards to fight over.

A bamboo building was seen a short distance away. We approached it with care. Suddenly, as we passed, a soldier walked out with rifle drawn. His language was of West Pakistan. We tried to explain that we were missionaries. We pointed in the direction we wanted to go. He walked with us to the dock.

The old shabby dock had not been harmed. But hundreds of other buildings which had stood nearby were debris and ashes. We started to walk by the dock. The soldier called to us and pointed to the dock. We followed his instructions and were led to an army Captain.

The Captain spoke good English. He was friendly and told us about the battle. We were pleased when he said, "These people are good fighters. We had a hard time taking this place." Bengalis were not the cowards some of the Pakistani military personnel spoke about.

It was twenty miles to Faridpur. The Captain said, "I have a vehicle coming in a few minutes. It will return to Faridpur. You may ride in it." We waited about two hours. Then I said to Phil, "Let's go! If we have to walk the entire distance, we may not be able to get there before darkness falls."

We started out walking. Just before we reached the main road, we saw a cycle rickshaw. The passenger got down. A soldier walked up to the rickshaw driver, and we saw him take something. When we reached the rickshaw, we found the driver deeply distressed. "What happened?" I asked. He replied, "The soldier took all of my money. I brought that passenger twelve miles and have had no lunch. Now what can I do?"

"Take us to the next road and I will repay what the soldier took and the regular fare," I said. Too weak to operate the rickshaw, the driver climbed into the seat with Phil. I tried to pedal the rickshaw. I leaned to the side as if I were on a bicycle. This did not work, and over an embankment we went.

Phil and the driver jumped out and I jumped off. We held on to the rickshaw, and no damage was done. I tried again and did a

53

little better. However I soon became tired. Phil and I pushed the rickshaw up the grades and rode downhill.

After about four miles, we found another rickshaw. We gave our driver sufficient money and moved on toward Faridpur. Soon we found another rickshaw and made the load lighter for each when we rode separately.

On that twenty mile journey, we counted houses that had been burned by the army. The dozens of little houses of most villages had been destroyed. Occasionally we noticed the army had left the better houses. At the end of the journey, we concluded that seventy-five percent of the houses had been burned.

When we approached Faridpur, I began considering what to say to the Rythers. I carried difficult news for them. I told Phil, "Let's wait until Carl is alone, and then he can tell Jean."

Though the circumstances were difficult, it surely was good to see that no harm had come to our two missionary families. After exchanging greetings with them, we all talked briefly about our families. The "choice" bit of news, perhaps, was that Gloria Thurman had delivered a Bengali baby boy shortly after the siege of Faridpur. They had named him Samson.

Soon after our arrival, Gloria went into the kitchen to prepare something to eat. Jean Ryther had already gone into a back room. This was perhaps the best time to deliver the message to Carl. My voice was too broken to produce, so I handed Carl the note which had come. "That's all I know," I remarked.

Though this was a severe blow to them, they took it like mature Christians. Carl said, "There is only one thing to do. We will go to Dacca tomorrow and on to West Pakistan immediately." I wanted to help. The Rythers had their place in East Pakistan in the midst of chaos. But the unexpected had happened. Their daughter needed them. They, without hesitating, made plans to join her.

That night we discussed in detail the events of the past few weeks. One shell had fallen on the Christian Industrial Center. The army had also burned one of the buildings of our Christian Agri-culture Center. For some reason that seemed to satisfy them, and they left the others.

The house in which the Joneses had lived bore several bullet marks. The army had practically destroyed the section of the town from which they had entered.

Tom said, "Many of the Bengali Christians fled and are still in hiding." As we talked, all of us were without words to describe the fear of the Bengalis in face of such brutal military power. Those not involved in the actual fighting often seemed to suffer most.

By daylight the next moning, Phil and I were walking with Carl, Jean and young Timothy Ryther toward the river. They were familiar with that area, and we were able to avoid the army at the dock.

We got into a large boat which was used for transporting cattle. We baked in the sun for several hours. After covering about half the distance back to our vehicle, we got a smaller boat for Jean and Timothy. Carl, Phil and I walked along the river bank for ten miles. When we reached the place where our vehicle was, we discovered that navy personnel had moved in, and they carefully checked our passports. No one was permitted to move about freely. We were all under strict military control.

Darkness came long before we reached Dacca. We were tired and sunburned. Just before we reached home we were traveling beside a high embankment. Suddenly a West Pakistan soldier pushed a Bengali policeman from the top of the embankment to the road right in front of our vehicle. He pointed his rifle to the front of the car. I slammed on the brakes and jumped out so that he could see I was a foreigner. I was sure he was ready to fire. The soldier laughed loudly.

I did not accept it as a joke. My anger kindled. I thought, "What would have happened had we been Bengalis?" I was helpless and the Bengalis were in a far worse condition.

Two days later, the Rythers left for West Pakistan. Upon arrival there, the Pakistan government gave them twenty-four hours to leave the country. The reason given was that their visas were not in order. Carla wasn't "emotionally ill." She was disturbed, but so were all missionary children who were separated from their parents. With only our two families in East Pakistan, the days ahead looked gloomy.

CHAPTER FIVE

Things could not have been worse. The departure of the Rythers crippled our spirits. The city of Dacca was still desolate. Daily, we saw trucks loaded with Bengali men being hauled away by the military. The stories concerning treatment of Bengali women mushroomed. Cherie and Kathy grew impatient.

Then two beautiful things happened. We met a Presbyterian couple at the International Church, Mr. and Mrs. Dale Wilkens, who soon became very dear friends. Later Mrs. Wilkens became Kathy's school teacher.

About a week after the Rythers left, the Thurmans moved to Dacca. This was the boost we needed. Philip and David, their sons, were smaller than Wade; but that made no difference. Cherie and Kathy, as well as our boys, received them with joy.

When I was in Faridpur, I wanted to ask the Thurmans to move to Dacca with us. However, I knew I did not have this right. They had responsibilities there; and living conditions were not too bad; and the border of India was at least sixty miles away. But the morning we left for Dacca, I had said to them, "If you want to come to Dacca, you will be more than welcomed by my family."

I believed they moved to Dacca, not because of their need, but because of our need for them. Kindness like this greatly assisted my family. God was at work, and we were being changed.

Tom and I appeared to have similar feelings about the brutality of the military against the Bengalis. Of course, this made our living together at the Guest House much easier.

The Thurmans had hardly arrived in Dacca when I began thinking that I should return to Feni and Comilla for a visit. The government radio was saying, "All is normal within the province of East Pakistan." I made plans for departure.

I drove the sixty miles to Comilla without any unusual difficulty. The Comilla Christians were somewhat surprised to see me. They thought we had left the country. The army was in full control, so I assumed the road on to Feni had been repaired enough for my vehicle to pass. I drove out of Comilla thinking the news "all is normal" applied to the border road.

However about ten miles south, I discovered that everything was anything but "normal." One village area was still smoking. Approximately two hundred houses had been burned. Bengalis ran as I approached this area. By the time I could stop and get out of the car, no one was in sight. The road was impassable.

I drove back a short distance to the village home of some Muslim friends. They gave their permission for my car to be left with them. We did our best to hide it, for I knew if the army found it in a border area, I would not see it again.

My Bengali friends helped me locate a cycle rickshaw. When I reached the area where the fire was still smoldering, a few Bengalis came toward my rickshaw. I got down and went to them. "What happened? Why did they do this?" I asked. The reply was, "The Freedom Fighters destroyed the bridge. Then the army came. They killed many of our people and burned our houses." I concluded, "If 'hell on earth' is normal, then everything in East Pakistan is normal."

Ordinarily the roads of Bangladesh are filled with people. Now along the remaining thirty mile route, only a few remained. They, too, were prepared to run across the border when the army came again.

Many of the Muslims felt that Allah was helping them because usually from November to the middle of June there is very little rain. Now, however, the hills of nearby India had filled the waterway with gushing water. This slowed the progress of the army and made houses more difficult to burn. One of the streams seemed impassable. The little bridge had been destroyed. A Freedom Fighter, with his rustic rifle, approached. "Oh, Sir," he said, "I will help you." He called out to friends nearby. They brought a small ferry-boat made of large banana stalks. We lifted the rickshaw carefully upon the ferry, and across the little stream it went.

"I hope to return tomorrow," I said. "Will you help me cross?" He kindly replied, "We are really sorry to cause you this trouble.

Tomorrow bring your rickshaw down this little path to our camp near the border. You can pass through it back to the main road."

About ten miles from where I left my vehicle, a Bengali called out as we passed. The rickshaw stopped. I got down as he approached, "Sir, may I ask, were you in the brown car, where the houses had been burned?" I answered, "Yes, but the people ran when I approached." "But we are really glad," he said, "we thought it was the army. I have been running along the road warning the people that the army may come. Now we can relax again." I was sorry so much trouble had struck because of my car. We talked about the pitiful condition of his war torn land, and then I moved on toward Feni.

I had decided to avoid the town of Feni by using the village road my family had traveled when we came out a few weeks ago. I did not want to be troubled by the army in town. Two miles out of Feni, at the place where I was to make the turn, the army had been posted.

I was ordered out of the rickshaw. As I got down, I said to the Bengali driver, "Don't be afraid. I can manage everything." I was wrong. The soldier thoroughly searched us and the rickshaw. He ordered us to sit down. It appeared that when I had spoken to the driver in Bengali, the soldier became angry because he did not understand Bengali. We had no way of explaining what I had said.

Also, since we had come the border road, he undoubtedly thought that we had come from India. I wondered how we could get out of this mess. After about thirty minutes, I discovered he had a telephone. I tried to request him to call an officer with whom I could talk in English. I succeeded by pointing to the telephone and pointing toward Feni.

He talked on the phone for a few minutes and then handed it to me. An army major was on the line. He couldn't seem to understand what I was doing on the border road. I finally remembered that maybe Mr. Belal, the West Pakistani civil government officer, was there. Then I asked, "May I speak to Mr. Belal?" He answered in what sounded as amazement, "Oh, so you know Mr. Belal. Yes, you may speak to him. He is here with me." Mr. Belal, too, was surprised. I explained where I was and that the soldier would not release me. He said, "I will speak to the major, and he will give you instructions." There was a pause. Then the major answered, "Come by your rickshaw directly to Mr. Belal's office. I will tell the soldier to release you." I handed the phone to the soldier and started walking toward the rickshaw. In a few minutes I was in the major's office.

Mr. Belal's appearance was greatly changed. It was apparent that he, too, was filled with fear. He was from an aristocratic West Pakistani family and did not "fit" very well with the military personnel around him. He asked about my family. He seemed surprised that the Bengalis had not harmed us and that I was able to travel freely. I, of course, could not tell him that I feared only the army.

The major listened to our conversation. Then he said, "When are you bringing your family back to Feni?" I replied, "I have no plans for bringing them back." "Oh, but you must," he answered; "everything is normal here." This was the classical lie of the times. Feni did not have one-fiftieth of its normal population. The people who were there, including even the apparent collaborators, were fear stricken. The major's army was brutal, and no one trusted them.

I began to feel he was trying to force me to bring Betty and the children back to Feni. I knew that our return to Feni would assist the army in its "all is normal" propaganda. If a foreign family could live there, then that would strengthen the army's claim. Moving back to Feni would have been collaboration with the army.

I tried to turn the conversation to lighter matters, but the major persisted in talking about our return to Feni. Finally I said, "If Mr. Belal will bring his family from West Pakistan and you will bring yours, then I will consider bringing my family." That was the end of talk of our return to Feni.

I wanted to leave, but Mr. Belal had to curse the Bengalis more, and the major continued questioning me. The major was interested in how I had come down the border road without any difficulty. His troops had not yet been able to do this. He asked me, "How many Indian soldiers did you see?" I answered, "Not any." "Then you must have seen their agents?" I again replied, "No, I did not see any Indian agents." The army had given the Bengali Freedom Fighters several names. One was "Indian Agents." They did not accept that the Bengalis fighting them were fighting for their own freedom.

I did not have to lie, for I had not seen any "Indian Agents." I had seen Freedom Fighters, but he did not ask me this.

After about one hour of questioning, I said, "I want to go on to my house before night." "Oh, yes, you must do this," the major said, "but aren't you afraid?" I was, but I replied, "No, everything will be okay." Then he said, "Why did you take the tires off your vehicles?" I answered, "I did not want anyone to take them." He replied, "We took them, but we had to break into your house to find the tires and the batteries." I quickly answered, "I hope you will return both vehicles immediately. One was for relief work, and the other vehicle is the one I use for my regular work. We do not want our vehicles used in killing people." I suppose my "little" sermon" didn't help, for he was only irritated by what I said.

A few minutes later the major said, "You may go." My ears burned as I walked away. Hearing roaring laughter from the major, I looked back. Some other officers had joined him. Though I was helpless to do anything, I was even more determined to make sure I did nothing to aid this army. I may have been to them "the little missionary who loves the natives," but I did begin to know for myself in a new way that I did love my Bengali friends and neighbors. I thought, "I will try to give them hope. Where possible, I will try to save their lives. This may be very little, but I am their friend."

It was May 6th. We had left Feni on April 14th. But what change had taken place! When we left, the Bengalis were ruling. Now the army was in full control. We had kept our yard neat right up to the day we left. Now the broken iron gate was lying in tall grass. Rather than break the lock, the army had broken down the gate. They had also broken into the house. Not even one person could be seen in our area of town. Yet the major had said, "Everything is normal." We may have been living in Dacca, but Feni was home. This house was our home.

Sultan, who had worked for us since our arrival in Feni in 1965, came just before darkness fell. It was helpful to see him alive, but he had no news of other friends. Sultan's face and lean body revealed the trying times. But his family in the village was okay.

The electricity had gone off a few days after our departure, so the deep-freeze and refrigerator were stinking with rotten food. Too bad, for some one needed that food; but there had been no way to save it. I had not eaten lunch that day, nor did I want to eat that night. I just went to bed early. As I lay in the bed trying to sleep, I concluded, "I will leave early in the morning if I can get past the army check-post."

Early the next morning, I told Sultan, "You must not stay

61

here. I will return soon and you will hear about it when I do, but you stay in the village. It does not matter about our things in the house."

After eating a light breakfast and filling my thermos with coffee, I stepped up into the rickshaw; and as it moved out toward the village road, I again looked back at our "home." It was no easier to leave this time.

As we moved on to the main road, the soldier motioned us by. That was a relief! I kept thinking as we rode along, "Sooner or later the army is going to take this area. I certainly hope it is not today."

Apparently the Freedom Fighters expected the army. They moved up to the road overnight. My progress was not hindered, however. In fact, they all seemed happy to see me, though I recognized only a few of them.

I chose not to accept the invitation to ride my rickshaw through their camp, but instead, crossed the little stream of water again on the stalk ferry.

At Noapara, about thirteen miles south of Comilla, one of the rickshaw tires burst. It took about an hour to get it repaired, and that hour was a difficult one. It was difficult because during that time I watched thousands of Bengalis cross the border road. They were coming from villages nearby and were moving quickly into India. The army was burning their houses to the West. Though I did not know it then, they were opening up a new road several miles from the border to link Comilla with the southern area of East Pakistan.

There was a solid line of Bengalis. They were loaded with meager possessions. Some led cows. Some led goats. Others pushed carts pulled by cows. Some were in rickshaws. Little children, with heavy burdens on their backs, cried as they struggled along. Generally, however, silence prevailed. Where were they going? To safety — they hoped. When would they return? No one knew. "Everything is normal in East Pakistan" according to the military government.

That line of "over-burdened" Bengalis halted for our rickshaw to pass. Eight or nine months later most of them would return with fewer possessions. Their bodies would be even weaker. They would have left many of their number in graves in India. They would return to the parched earth on which their houses had stood. But they would return to a free land.

62

My car was okay. But my village friends were glad to see it leave. They had been true friends for I had asked a lot. The army would· have caused them difficulty had they found the vehicle this near the border. Eight months passed before I traveled the Comilla/Feni road again because that road became a continuous battle area.

Mrs. Roy, who with her family had been so gracious to us when we came out of Feni three weeks earlier, was again a perfect hostess. She fed me well that night. Others joined her family, and we talked long about what all of us would do. Mrs. Roy said, "Mr. McKinley, except for my oldest son, I think I will send all of my family to India for safety. What do you think?" My reply was of little help for I said, "I must not make any suggestions. I will support all of you in your decisions and will help whenever possible, but I must not say what I think you should do."

She seemed to understand. This was no time to offer advice. This was a time for all to decide for themselves and for others to support. That continued to be my position for the duration of the Bengali freedom struggle.

I slept in the Buckleys' house again. Early the next morning I moved on toward Dacca to join Betty, our children and the Thurmans.

I soon learned that screaming could be beautiful. Every time I returned from Comilla and Feni during the civil war, I was greeted with a scream from the children, "Daddy! Daddy! Mother, Daddy has come back!" Kathy's highly pitch voice was always heard over the others.

It was good once again to have the assurance I feel in the presence of my family. I gave them the details of the entire journey. The children were especially concerned about their little Bengali friends in Feni, but I had no news about them. They were all either hiding in villages or in India.

Tom and I discussed what we should do about trying to hold our work together. We had suddenly dipped from seven families on the field to two families. The military government was giving pressure for all work to continue. We had to decide how much to do in order for our presence to appear necessary and to consider the livelihood of all those related to our organization. We accepted the fact that not much work could be done in this situation.

We also decided that we would travel together outside Dacca. It seemed that the presence of the second person might have value in the event of trouble. Since I had just returned from Feni and Comilla, it was natural that we should go to Faridpur.

Travel to Faridpur in May was easier than to Feni. The India border made the difference. The Faridpur people, especially the Christians, were excited at seeing Tom. Many of them thought the Thurmans had gone to Dacca and had left the country. The town of Faridpur was somewhat "normal."

The Rythers had been using a new pickup truck in Carl's agriculture work. The army had taken the truck and used it as an ambulance. They had not used it for a few days, however. When Tom and I started for Dacca, we took the truck. The army made no inquiry about it.

Pleasant screams from our children greeted us when we reached the Guest House. Those screams again meant strength — strength to "go again" on what I believed was God's mission.

The latter part of May, Tom and I departed for Comilla and Feni. In Comilla we learned that the new road, several miles inland from the Indian border, was open. As we proceeded toward Feni, we did find the road open; but our vehicle hardly made the trip because of broken motor supports destroyed as we attempted to "jump" some of the rough spots.

I now understood why the thousands of Bengalis had poured across the border at Noapara on my previous trip. When the army moved in to open the new road, they had burned thousands of houses. Then, too, when we first came from Feni to Comilla, the heavy shelling we heard had been in this area. Large markets had become parched earth except for occasional vacant brick buildings. We saw a few Bengalis. All were distinctly marked with fear.

Choumuhani is the largest business area of Noakhali. Business never entered our minds as we drove through. The main area had been burned, and crumbled rusty tin and ashes characterized the market. We had an evangelistic center in Choumuhani. Would it ever be reopened?

The army had set up a check post one mile west of our house. They delayed us only momentarily. Everything was "becoming normal." Foreigners were traveling.

Feni was still more like a ghost town. Sultan had returned to our house, however. I learned that of the six local people working with us, five of them had lost almost everything they owned. Four of them had fled to India with their families.

The army major was angry. Mr. Belal had left Feni and, according to the major, had gone to West Pakistan. The major was having difficulty trying to make the "normal" situation without the civil official.

There was little reason for lingering in Feni. What could we do? Nothing — but maybe someday there would be a change. But how long, that someday? Early the next morning Tom and I started back toward Dacca. Soon after we turned on the new road at Choumuhani, we came upon a three-wheeled motor scooter which had broken down. The rough road was too much for the little overloaded vehicle.

One of the passengers came to us saying, "May I accompany you to Comilla and even to Dacca if you are going that far?" I replied, "We are quite willing for you and your companions to ride with us." His companions and the men from Feni who were already with us filled the two back seats of the microbus. This apparently educated gentleman rode in the front with Tom and me.

He lost no time in identifying himself. "I am a member of the Central Peace Committee," he said. My first reaction was to spit in his face and accept the consequences. "Peace Committees" were being established throughout East Pakistan by the military government. While I did have deep sympathy for some of those who had been forced to become members, I knew that anyone who boasted of membership was a collaborator with the army. Here I was permitting a traitor against his own people, the Bengalis, to ride in my vehicle.

But what else could I do? I had chosen to stay in East Pakistan. If I put him out of the car, no doubt, I would soon be on my way back to the States. But if Tom and I were compromising, we tried to make up for it.

More villages had been burned. From some areas where the smoke still swirled, pathetic poor Bengalis ran out to the road screaming at the two white faces, "Please help us! They are killing us!" Tom and I well knew who was killing them, but I asked, "Who is doing this?" "The army! The army!" came the reply. "Please tell the world!" they pleaded. "We will do all we can to tell of your troubles," I answered.

The "gentleman" riding with us squirmed each time we stopped to talk with the suffering Bengalis. It was difficult to believe he could hate his own people so much.

Every time we stopped, we heard the same pleas and replied in the same manner. However, in our efforts to impress upon our passenger the tragedy, we often repeated, "Who is doing this?" and "We will do all we can to tell of your troubles."

Tom came through beautifully. He made every effort to expose the tragedies being committed along this one road. His sympathy for the Bengalis was deep. So he also spoke openly in front of this "Peace Committee" member. He watched the villages more carefully since I was driving. When he saw that houses had been burned he said, "Look, Jim, look! The people are coming. Stop, let's listen to them." Our passenger was really paying for his ride.

But neither was he silent. On several occasions he said, "But they deserve this. They are no good. They are Indian agents." Such remarks brought replies from Tom and me, "But they are not Indians. This is their home. They only want to be free."

Sometimes as we bounced along on the rough road, our passenger dozed. When he did, we tried to draw his attention to the suffering of his own people. We gave him no rest in our vehicle. He had to, at least for the time with us, accept our reminders of the atrocities against the Bengalis.

In Comilla, while Tom and I visited with the Bengali Christians, our passengers visited with local "Peace Committee" members.

On the previous trip I had made alone to Feni, everything was peaceful between Comilla and Dacca. So as we left Comilla, I pondered our situation. "Were we over doing it? Were we going outside our role of missionaries as guests in another country? Did we have a right to be so hard on this man, who was a part of the present government?

But our pressure on this passenger increased about twenty-five miles west of Comilla. At this point, not only the border area but inland areas also were coming under the hard hand of the army. Suddenly we came upon soldiers with machine guns set up on the road. We slowed down but were motioned on. Then we speeded up again. But a short distance away we found ourselves in the midst of a "shoot-out" between the army and the Bengalis. Mortars were pointed toward villages on both sides of the road. Soldiers were lying flat on the pavement with guns pointed toward the villages. We could not pass.

Our passenger shouted, "Oh, those poor soldiers! They are enduring so much for us!" I screamed, "The poor village people! How can they endure this suffering?"

A truck was filled with blind-folded Bengalis who were being beaten by the soldiers. Blood flowed from their faces.

66

An army officer began rebuking us. I replied, "We have been told that everything is normal. There are no restrictions on our traveling as foreigners." He did not agree. "You have no right to be on the roads. You may get into trouble," he said. "These are dangerous days," he continued.

Then he asked for our passports. We showed them; but then he said, "Who are all of these people?" I replied, "They live here in East Pakistan. They have their identifications." He examined the luggage of each passenger and carefully read their identification papers. He compared the photographs on the identifications.

It did not seem to be all that dangerous for the soldiers. The officer stood by our vehicle for at least fifteen minutes. The "shoot-out", it seemed was going in only one direction. The only problem with our presence on this road was that we had caught the army assaulting a village of poor uneducated people. Yes, they probably had been told that Freedom Fighters were hiding in those villages.

But as we were released and drove on, Bengalis with tattered and torn clothes called out to us to stop. We stopped. "They are killing us! We have done nothing!" came the desperate cries. Our passenger did not reply. Then I said to him, "Sir, your identification is useless. At the rate this army is going, they will kill you also; you are a Bengali." I could not understand. How could a man be so blind? The only halfway reasonable conclusion I could reach was that he was a politician. His party had "lost everything" in the previous election. But now he saw an opportunity to become "somebody" again under the military government. But what a price to pay!

When he got out of our vehicle, I gave him my calling card saying, "If you ever need me, you can inquire at this address." Though I expected he would do something against Tom and me, I have not seen him since that day. He was later elected a member of the National Assembly of Pakistan replacing a person who fled from the army. I also later learned that before Bangladesh was liberated, he fled and went abroad to live.

Today I can only wish for an opportunity to talk to this man and others like him. I want to share how God helped me overcome hatred. He can help them overcome the same.

Those beautiful screams greeted Tom and me again as we reached the Guest House. If everything were normal, we were deaf, dumb, and blind. There was suffering, and I was glad God had let me share a little in it.

CHAPTER SIX

The trip Tom and I made to Comilla and Feni was the last time we rode outside of Dacca in the same vehicle. Though we felt no one was after us, there was apparent danger. We were the only two men in our organization. So from that time on, usually one of us traveled while the other stayed with our families at the Guest House.

Tom and Gloria decided to go to Faridpur and leave their sons with us. Their trip was chaotic. Since they were traveling by public conveyance, progress was slower and at times quite uncertain. On the return trip they were caught at one of the rivers at night. Eventually, they were able to travel two miles to a town where the only place for them to spend the night was upstairs in a building occupied downstairs by the Pakistan army.

Naturally, there was little rest that night. They proceeded slowly toward Dacca early the next morning. Near Dacca they watched in horror as jet planes of the Pakistan Air Force strafed villages. They left the main road and entered Dacca from the villages. When they reached the Guest House, their weary appearance revealed the troubles they had endured.

Gloria remarked, "This is the last time we will leave without the boys." In times of danger, if at all possible, I wanted my family together. I felt security for myself and them when we were together, for it seemed that we were stronger when we could depend upon one another. Then, too, when I considered that something might happen to us, I seemed to want it to happen to all of us. It appeared that the Thurmans, too, wanted to face danger together.

But in my traveling, I made one exception to this. Keith often wanted to go back "home" to Feni with me. I refused to take him over the road from Comilla to Feni.

Though I was often naive to danger, I knew the Comilla/Feni inland road was dangerous. I was really shaken when I first discovered this danger. I was traveling the road alone. Suddenly I came upon a huge hole in the road. Without thinking, I got out of my vehicle and filled the hole with brick so that I could drive on.

A short distance away village people ran as I approached. I quickly stopped, jumped out, and shouted to them in Bengali, "Come back! I am your friend! I will not cause you any harm!" They stopped and slowly came to me.

I asked, "Why did you run?" "Oh, Sir, we thought you were a soldier," they replied. I asked, "Why is the big hole in the road?" The answer came quickly and with pathos, "Oh, Sir, please be careful. That hole was made by a road mine. An army jeep was blown to pieces by it. Didn't you see those pieces?"

I walked back to the hole. There was deep water on each side of the road. Of course, I could not see all of the jeep pieces. Of those I saw, however, none were more than six inches long. There was no sign of blood or human flesh. Those soldiers never knew what hit them. My body turned cold. I trembled with fear. I thought, "I'll not travel this road again."

I quietly gave a "Salaam" to the men with whom I had talked and drove on. But I drove slowly. Men were dying. "Was I ready to die? Was the reason for keeping my family in this land justifiable? What would be my attitude if my leg or both legs were blown off by a lesser mine?" Forgetting at times that my vehicle might even then strike a mine, I continued to ponder the situation.

This was the area where so many houses had been burned. There were few people to be seen. The scorched earth seemed to cry out as I drove on. Someone who had seen, not just heard, needed to be in the free world telling the story. Should I not do this rather than simply remain in East Pakistan where most of the time I could do absolutely nothing but listen to tales of horror and sorrow?

In Feni, Sultan said, "The Major often comes by asking where you are and what you are doing. I only tell him I don't know but that you are a good man and that you won't harm anyone; but that does not satisfy him."

The monsoon rains were beginning to fall. The roads were becoming more difficult to travel. There was nothing to do in Feni

70

after I spoke to the few friends who were still there. The next day I started back toward Dacca.

Enroute I met a convoy of military vehicles. One of them sunk down into the soft earth. I was delayed for about two hours. I talked with the soldiers. Their broken English was difficult to understand, but it was our only language for communication. I asked them, "Where are your guns from?" They laughed, "The new ones are Chinese but no good. The old ones are English — many years old — but better than new Chinese ones." I especially wanted to know whether or not they were receiving new small weapons from my country. Apparently, they were not.

When the road was open for me to drive on, I discovered my vehicle was stalled in the mud. I motioned for the soldiers to push. They called out in English to a few Bengalis standing nearby, "Push the white man's car. He is your friend." They did not understand English but knew why they had been called. They pushed without hesitating. In Bengali, I thanked them and said, "Truly, I am your friend." The sign of friendship broke through faces strained by fear and hatred. They were afraid of the army. They hated the army. But those soldiers knew of my sympathy for the Bengalis!

In Comilla, I picked up Father Young, two Bengali Catholic sisters and two other Bengalis. At an army check-post the guard asked, "Are these members of your family?" Rather than confuse the issue, I replied, "yes, they are." We drove on. I thought to myself, "I answered correctly. They are members of my family. Ours is a family of deep friendship in the midst of great suffering." Foreign Catholic Fathers throughout East Pakistan were clearly identified with the suffering Bengalis. Many of them were my friends.

The usual screams greeted me at the Guest House.

The city of Dacca was taking on new sounds. Regularly, bombs exploded shattering electric transmission stations and other vital installations.

Though we were often without electricity, there were no complaints. The Freedom Fighters of Bangladesh were making their presence known.

In the midst of this, Tom could nearly always be counted on for a good strengthening laugh. Quite often when our two families were sitting together at night, there would be a blast. The lights would go out with the blast. Each time Tom quietly remarked, "Hold on to your purses, ladies."

The most relaxing time, however, was watching Tom while he watched T.V. news. The news itself was sickening. It was totally propaganda. Tom preferred the rocking chair. He wanted complete quiet. Then, as the news progressed, he continually rocked and talked, saying, "Well, I didn't see it like that . . . Oh, you don't say . . . Well, how could you arrive at that . . . Yes, everything is normal. . . ." The longer the news lasted, the faster Tom rocked and the more comments he made.

Then as we prepared to go to bed, Tom often remarked, "Since all is normal, we need not fear. Sleep in peace." Sometimes this was followed by a trembling explosion. Tom again would come through, "Well, wonder what that little noise was? Some child must be playing with fire crackers!"

Often when an explosion shook the house, Tom and his family had already gone upstairs to bed. Tom would come back down, knock on our bedroom door, then ask with a straight face, "Did you hear anything?" Other times, he would come down and whisper, "Joi Bangla (victory for the Bengalis) and then quietly return upstairs. On many occasions my children said, "Daddy, Uncle Tom is wonderful, isn't he?" He was.

I found myself wanting our house and belongings in Feni to survive. Ian McDonald, who was with a British relief agency, used the house for some of his men. No one was about to take anything when Ian was around! His men were involved in cultivating with tractors, so the Freedom Fighters were not opposed to what they were doing since this would not aid the army. But Ian's men were there for only a short time.

An American engineer also stayed in the house for a time. I was more cautious about him. He was working on small bridges south of Feni. But after carefully considering the situation, I felt it was okay. The Bengalis with whom I discussed his work said, "The job he is doing will not be completed for several years. By that time we will be free and will need the bridges. But, on the other hand, if freedom is delayed, we won't let the bridges be completed."

This engineer was fearless. Five hundred Razakars, non-Bengali and Bengali collaborators who had been formed into a paramilitary force, camped across the road from our house. They took away some of our things while the engineer was at the bridge sites.

When Sultan told him what had happened, he created an impressive scene.

The engineer walked into camp kicking over chairs and screaming in English. They didn't understand his words. But everything was returned. They took nothing else.

Those Razakars were gutless. They had courage only when accompanied by the army or when they pointed their guns at unarmed Bengalis. They were traitors to the people of Bangladesh and were marked by cowardice. But they created havoc, especially in village areas. Brutality was their distinguishing characteristic, but the looting of valuables of the poor wasn't far behind. They did, however, leave our house alone after the lone American engineer displayed his courage.

Some Feni people prepared to entertain a former politician who was associated with the actions of the Pakistan army. They decided the best place to find nice dishes was in our house. They helped themselves to what they wanted over Sultan's objection. But, to Sultan's surprise, they returned everything.

In 1965, when we had lived in Comilla, this politician had come there to make a public speech. The Comilla students had refused to let him speak because they accused him of betraying East Pakistan in favor of West Pakistan. We had watched as many of the students jumped the fence into our yard with blood squirting from their hands and faces after being beaten by the para-military forces of that time. He had spoken that day, but it had been brief. He later died in jail in Free Bangladesh in 1973.

On one occasion while in Feni, I was told to come to the office of the local "Peace Committee" chairman. I had no choice but to go. But I feared I would be asked to serve on the committee. It would have been impressive to say, "All is normal" if a missionary were a "Peace Committee" member. I went to the office.

In flowering words, the chairman began telling me about how stable the military government was. He had been one of the two people who refused to help us get permission for a hospital in Feni several years before.

But as he talked, I learned much about how he really felt. He asked me, "When is your family returning to Feni?" I replied, "Maybe never." I suspected the Major had given him the responsibility of getting my family back to Feni. If so, the chairman failed. That's the last thing I would do. Actually this wasn't the chairman's real feeling. Before the conversation ended, he said to me, "Please take my family to Dacca the next time you come to Feni. This is a dangerous place to live." He continued, "I don't know what I am going to do." I agreed.

When I went to take his wife and children the next trip back to Feni, the chairman was not there. Friends told me that he had left a few days earlier with his family. The last report I heard of him was that he fled at the time of liberation and his whereabouts were still unknown.

CHAPTER SEVEN

Cherie and Kathy continued to draw attention to my family's presence in Dacca. What were two attractive little foreign girls doing in East Pakistan at such a time of horror?

The Bengali reaction was usually a "Thank you for staying with us." The reaction of foreign men, most of whom were present without their wives — much less their children, was often quite different. Some went so far as to say, "You are foolish for keeping your family here." Others said, "You have no right to do this. You don't understand what may be happening to your children."

The person who really helped us was Rev. Leslie Wenger, our British Baptist missionary friend, who was born in old India. He had gone back to Britain for his education. Later he returned to India and eventually to East Pakistan. He had served in these areas thirty-one years as a missionary.

Mr. Wenger, as we all called him, as Pastor of the Dacca International Christian Church, took a special interest in our children. They looked forward to his visits. Early in the crisis, he told Betty and me, "Watch Wade carefully. He is young and probably will not be able to express his feelings. Reassure him of your love and always let him talk."

We took Mr. Wenger's words seriously. I had been primarily concerned about Cherie and Kathy. Maybe it was because I felt they would blame me if anything happened to one of us. But I also knew there was real danger for them. Pakistani soldiers continued their brutality. This was vividly expressed in their pagan behavior toward young Bengali women.

My concern for Wade increased. He had talked very little. Usually a smile covered his freckled face. I had to ask myself,

"Does he understand what is happening? Does he think about the people who are being treated like animals?" He said little other than when he prayed, "Dear God, bless the Bengalis. Help them. Don't let them suffer."

I never had to wonder about Keith. Everyone always knew how he felt. He seemed to express every thought. He wanted to travel with me and see first hand what was happening. But I didn't want him to see any more horror.

I had never bought either of my sons a toy gun. It troubled me when they had fights with their little friends. My feelings about violence of any type increased. The word itself became repulsive to me. But here I was, choosing to keep my family in the midst of violence, when they could have been in America with kind, loving grandparents.

There were times, especially during the first three months of the civil war, when I felt that perhaps those who expressed criticism to me about my keeping my family in East Pakistan were right. Betty and I often talked about whether or not things were happening to the children which we could not see. As the struggle for Bengali freedom continued, more foreigners began to return, especially to Dacca, though very few brought their families. I was pleased to hear some of them say, "The children seem to be doing great." This helped, for it gave me badly needed assurance.

Even still, I had to ask, "Was simply remaining justifiable? What was I doing that was of value?" Our organization owned property in four cities of East Pakistan. The value of this might have been as much as $400,000.00. If my family departed and the Thurmans also chose to leave, we might lose all of that property. I could have remained and sent my family out, but I did not believe I could remain alone for a long period. The question then was — should I keep my family in a land of civil war just to protect property? The answer was — no.

A seemingly more important reason for remaining was that often when a missionary organization tries to enter a country, there are difficulties relating to visas and other restrictions. As long as we remained, we would not be on the outside wishing we were in the country. I ruled that out, however, as a simple logical reason for keeping the children in a war-torn land.

The answer was that this was God's mission for us as a family. He called us to this land. Our children gladly accepted their relationships with Bengali children. The tragic November, of 1970, had drawn all of us nearer to the Bengalis. The days in Feni during March and April of 1971 deepened this relationship. Freedom-loving Bengalis seemed to want us. Remaining, at times, was not easy. But departing would have been even more difficult.

The Guest House doors were open to anyone who wanted to come by and talk. People from all walks of life came. Among them were Mrs. Guha and her daughter. Professor Guha, her husband and an outstanding Hindu teacher of Dacca University, had been killed by the soldiers on March 26th. A kind American friend brought them to visit with Betty, Cherie and Kathy. We were strengthened from the visit of people like these who were suffering so much.

On some occasions, Bengalis seemed to come in from the street without any purpose. Often they spoke openly of hatred harbored within their souls. Fear was deep and the future dark to most of them. We assured them, as best we could, that someday they would experience freedom. Some sat for a long time talking rapidly. Suddenly they would get up and say, "I must go." Many of those we never saw again.

If what we were doing were wrong, we did not question it at that time. We knew that in the past some missionaries had reportedly been watched by the Security Police. I did not question whether or not we were being watched. We knew well that we had no right to political involvement. We were foreigners. But any government knows that missionaries are concerned about inhuman treatment of people regardless of who those people are. It seemed to me that if we could not express kindness, if we could not encourage people, if we could not help protect them, if we could not oppose violence, we had no mission in East Pakistan or anywhere else.

Ray Schaefer, of the Australian Baptist Mission, was at the Guest House several times. He asked me in May if I would go with him to Pabna. Pabna was about one hundred miles northeast of Dacca. The military had taken one of their vehicles, and he was trying to recover it. I was glad to make the trip with Ray, to be his traveling companion, and to drive the vehicle back to Dacca.

The last twelve miles of the route we saw that the army had been just as brutal in that area. Houses, by the dozens, had been burned. Even some of the large brick structures in the city lay in shambles. The few Christians remaining in Pabna were, as others, marked by a deep fear. Each one had no idea of what the next day might bring.

77

We had a worship service on the back porch of a vacated missionary residence. The service was informal and deeply meaningful to all of us.

While we were in Pabna, I often looked out the front windows of the residence and gave thanks to God that the missionaries who had lived there before March 25, 1971, had been able to escape along with many Bengalis into India.

It seemed to me that God's miracle had worked for all of us on His mission. Some had fled across the border into India. Their going was a report to the world that East Pakistan was being brutally battered by military forces. It was an unfit place to live.

A few of us were able to remain because of a difference of geography. We were given the mission of sharing with suffering Bengalis. Even the thoughts of how some of our fellow missionaries must have endured those early days gave us the strength we needed. There was no doubt — God was at work in Bangladesh. Surely the missionary force of the future would be a more dedicated group.

Samson Chowdhury, a leading businessman in Pabna, had been a long time friend. We had attended a missions conference in Hong Kong almost ten years before the beginning of the atrocities. Ray and I visited with him and his family. Samson was a different man as he talked. He told us, "We were in our village home when the army came along the road you traveled into Pabna. Seeing the burning of houses and hearing the shelling, we fled into the interior. The army followed us and hundreds of others. Some fell when strength gave out. We continued and the army eventually turned back to the main road. As things quietened, we came back."

Samson continued, "Now, what will happen, we do not know. Two of my sons have fled, and I assume they are Freedom Fighters. I expect my youngest son to slip away and join them at any moment." I noticed that the youngest son had very little to say while we were there. He later left home and joined the Freedom Fighters. Before the civil war ended, Samson had joined his sons.

Ray did not get his vehicle that trip. But our journey had not been wasted. We had talked with friends; that was enough.

Each time I traveled out of Dacca, hate seemed to build up in my heart. I didn't like this, but overcoming it was not easy. As a family we talked about this danger. When we prayed, we asked God to help us. I found that hate is horrible for a Christian. My hate was directed against the Pakistan military forces and those collaborating with them. Often when I prayed I said, "Oh, God, can I not truly love the Bengalis without hating the Pakistanis?"

While in Feni on one trip, a friend told me about the "Reception Center" for Bengali refugees supposedly returning from India. These "Reception Centers" were being set up in several places near the border to receive those who came back to "normal" East Pakistan.

"The fact is," my friend said, "five hundred people were brought here to pose as returned refugees. Not even one of them had gone to India." While the outside would read about refugees returning to East Pakistan, I knew it was all a big lie.

I shared the Feni experience with a representative of the United Nations High Commissioner for Refugees. I doubted that he believed my story. I could have told him more, but it didn't seem to me to be of any value.

My good friend in Feni also told me that on one occasion a few refugees did return from India. Among them was a Hindu lady. She was kept at the "Reception Center" overnight and was raped several times. Her screams were heard all night. I chose to believe my friend, but this only increased the hatred.

A young army Captain in Feni caused my hatred to grow even more. This Captain was extremely intelligent. He spoke several languages; and even though he was from West Pakistan, Bengali was one of those languages. He was strikingly handsome. I went to him because a Christian family trying to live in Feni was being constantly harrassed by the soldiers. Mr. Sircar, the Christian friend, had told me, "The soldiers walk through our house at any and all hours taking what few things we have, but I fear most for my little daughters."

Before I told the Captain the purpose of my visit to him, he began asking me questions about Feni. "How many Christians live here?" I answered, "Only two families." He asked, "Where are they now?" I replied, "One family went to India, I understand." In louder words he asked, "But why did they run away? Did they fear us?" I answered, "I am sure they feared you."

In a loud voice filled with anger he said, "Where is the other family?" I replied, "They are in Feni, but life is very difficult for them." He then stormed, "What's wrong? I am now in charge here." I said, "Your men regularly go to their houses and take what they please. That family is living in constant fear."

He jumped to his feet and said, "What men? Not my men."

I answered, "Yes, your men. Men like those standing here by you." The Captain was in charge of a group of West Paskistanis who had been recruited from the tribal border areas. They had grown up with rifles in their hands. They had been filled with propaganda in route to East Pakistan. So to them, every Bengali, except the few collaborators, was an Indian Hindu agent. These men were huge and rugged in appearance. Even the sight of them caused most Bengalis to tremble.

They had taken over our Evangelistic Center in Feni. A Muslim Bengali young man told them, "Those books on which you are walking are the Christian's Holy Book." The young man reported to me, "They laughed when I told them and kicked the Bibles across the floor." But someday more Bibles could be bought. Mr. Sircar's family was now my concern.

My accusation against the Captain's men had been strong. But he talked on telling how the Bengalis were destroying Pakistan. "Some of those people even fire on my soldiers," he shouted "and when they do, I burn their villages. I will burn more if anyone fires at my soldiers."

I did not tell the Captain that Mr. Sircar's wife and two oldest daughters were living in a village because of fear. I also did not tell him about his soldiers' treatment of our Evangelistic Center, which served as our place of worship.

But my mission again wasn't a failure. Before I departed, he said, "I have two friends at the military hospital in Dacca. I want you to visit them and bring news of them when you come to Feni again." Though his request had sounded like a command, I felt that if I wanted to help the Sircars and if I were ever going to return to Feni, I must do as he had requested.

Since Keith had so much wanted to share more with me, I took him to the military hospital. His presence helped. We had no difficulty entering the army base. The two officers whom we were going to visit had been injured just outside of Feni. This was further proof to us that the Freedom Fighters of Bangladesh were continuing their struggle.

The major had severe flesh wounds. "No more of this war for me. I will be flown home in a few days. After recovery, I will probably receive a medical discharge. And I surely am glad to be getting out of here." I chose to believe what I heard him say — "I don't like what is happening here." He seemed to be kind.

The Captain in the bed next to the Major's was in a more serious condition. Among other injuries, his neck was broken. He said nothing, but smiled at Keith.

Just before Keith and I left, the Major said, "Those Feni people of yours are tough fighters. They almost got us. We are all surprised at the way they are resisting." I liked the "of yours." He associated us with the Bengalis and yet was kind to us. As we departed, he said to Keith, "Keith, when you grow up, be an engineer or a doctor or even a missionary like your father. But don't be a soldier."

Keith and I walked to the car. Both of us were well aware that not all the soldiers involved in the atrocities against the Bengalis were in favor of what was happening. Some were very much opposed but could do nothing about it. They were only obeying orders.

I felt better inside as we drove back to the Guest House some five miles away. God had helped. For sure my hatred had been tested. I had no feelings against those officers. And it wasn't simply because they were no longer involved in the war.

The next trip to Feni I inquired about the Captain who had requested me to visit his friends in the Dacca hospital. He had been promoted and transferred.

But on the same journey, I met another officer who was in charge of a Special Forces group. He said he had been trained several years ago in Key West, Florida, and Panama. He talked freely, so I did also. "Do you have a family?" I asked. "No, came the reply, but I surely want to go home so I can get married." I said, "You and I share the same feelings; I also want you to go home."

"Oh," he replied, "You missionaries are too holy." "But," he said, "I am also opposed to what is happening here." He continued, "These people do not want us. Why should we want to remain here, much less kill them?"

I said, "Then why don't you go home?" He replied, "You know better than that; I can't go home. If I did, I would be court-martialed." I admitted, "Yes, I know that, but I surely am glad you are at least opposed to what is happening here." He assured me, "I am opposed."

Many Pakistani soldiers would never go home. Grave markers lined the banks of two ponds in Feni. Though thousands of Bengalis were dying, Pakistani soldiers were also dying. The Pakistan President, who never came to East Pakistan during the war, continued to say, "All is normal."

This officer had pulled away a chunk of my hatred. The President of Pakistan, the Commander of those forces, continued putting it back, so my struggle continued.

Often I found myself wondering what had happened to Mr. Alam, my family's friend and the "diplomat turned farmer." Had he been killed by the army in route to his home in Chittagong? I discovered myself asking the question when I traveled and saw soldiers brutally mistreating Bengalis. But relief came. We heard on the Free Bangladesh radio station that Mr. Alam had become the Foreign Secretary of the newly formed Bangladesh government. The Bengali leader, Sheik Mujibur Rahman, was still reported to be in prison in West Pakistan, but others continued the struggle. I felt the new government was fortunate to have men of the character and intelligence of Mr. Alam. We prayed more for freedom for Bangladesh.

The Christian young men who worked with us in our five Evangelistic Centers of Noakhali scattered when the army came into Feni in April. A few of them returned later, and we kept three of the centers open part of the time for those who wanted to come and talk.

Bidhan, one of those young men, and I went to visit our Center in Choumuhani. We discovered it had been taken over by the "Peace Committee". The man jumped to his feet when we walked in. On racks where we had kept Gospel tracts, rifles were hanging. Of course, he recognized us; but he asked, "Who are you? What right do you have to come in here?"

Without hesitating I answered, "You know who we are. This is our building. We have it legally leased. Just what right do *you* have here?" This caught him off guard. He had not expected such an answer.

I said, "I insist on seeing the person responsible for this. You have made our holy place a military office. This is where our Bibles are kept and read." "But we only work here," came the feeble reply. I asked, "How can you call yourselves 'Peace Committee' when you take away our Bibles and replace them with rifles?" He gave no reply.

Bidhan and I learned that our center was being used to issue rifles to new members of the collaborating force, the Razakars. The building was owned by a Hindu who had fled to India. All of our supplies were eventually destroyed.

82

Confusion was the most common experience. We had not heard anything from Professor Majumder, our friend from Feni, since I saw him in early April. We assumed he had escaped to India with his family and was serving with the Bangladesh Government.

Disappointment, however, came to our family when early one evening the children were watching television. They called out, "Daddy, come quickly." I ran to where they were watching television. "Who is that man, Daddy?" the children asked. I could hardly believe what I was seeing. "It's Professor Majumder," I replied.

"But, Daddy, he looks so different," Cherie said, "And why is he on television? The army doesn't like him."

"Maybe he was caught by the army and is being forced to make the speech," was my reply. I listened carefully to what he said in Bengali. He didn't seem natural, but most people aren't when on television. He was speaking on the life of a famous Bengali who had started the political party of Sheik Mujibur Rahman. The speech seemed out of place. It was another move by the military government to feed propaganda to the Bengalis. My family only wondered what had happened to this man.

We liked Professor Majumder. He had been kind to our family in Feni. He had been popular with students in Feni. He was respected by most people in our town. "What could have happened?" we wondered.

The next trip to Feni, I inquired from a friend, "What has happened to our professor friend?" The reply came, "Oh, him, we don't understand. He went to India. He came back to East Pakistan. He is now a minister in the puppet Governor's cabinet." The friend continued, "I saw him recently but was afraid to ask too many questions. He said he knew you were in Dacca but that he had never gone to visit with you."

We never learned what happened. When Bangladesh was freed in December 1971, he was taken prisoner. He was later tried and given a life sentence.

The experience was confusing to me. It was even more confusing to the children. The only conclusion we reached was — civil war does terrible things to the minds of men. The physical destruction is only a part of the tragedy.

Of Bengali Muslim leaders whom I knew on March 25, 1971, Professor Majumder drew my respect along with Mr. Alam and Rab Chaudhury. The professor had apparently, for some reason, gone over to the side of the enemy of the Bengalis. Mr. Alam was the Foreign Secretary of the Bangladesh Government in exile. But my frindship with Rab grew.

Rab was in the tidal wave disaster area when March 25 came. He had miraculously reached his family in Dacca. Soon after we came to Dacca in April, I visited with him. I had no doubt where he stood. He was a true Bengali; he wanted freedom for Bangladesh. His position was a difficult one, however. He was a government Civil Service Officer. His movements were being watched.

The office of which he was now in charge was not very important. It was apparent to me why he had been given this position. He often spoke of his desire to get out of East Pakistan and try to raise support abroad for Bangladesh. I only listened to his remarks. His family ties were strong. Perhaps this is what kept him in East Pakistan during 1971.

But the change in him during that year revealed the tragic suffering of Bangladesh. He was capable enough to represent his people ably to any country, but in this situation he was almost helpless. I felt one responsibility to him — I continually encouraged him to believe that Bangladesh would some day be free.

Late one night Rab honored our friendship by bringing reporters, Loren Jenkins of *Newsweek* and Dan Coggin of *Time,* to the Guest House for a visit. This was the beginning of many occasions through which I was able to share my impressions of what was happening to the Bengalis.

Though often I guarded what I said, usually I felt the reporters could be trusted. On one occasion a reporter introduced himself as a representative of an internationally known encyclopedia. That was too much for me. I suggested that if this were his true role, he should come at a more normal time. I did not trust him though this may have been his legitimate role.

But among all of the reporters, we admired Sidney Schaneburg of *The New York Times* most. He and Tom became close friends. Their friendship gave my family opportunity to be with Sidney. I admired him because the Bengali struggle became his struggle. Once we talked until midnight about what was happening in Bangladesh. From the conversation with the Thurmans, Betty and me, he could have written several stories. Of course, this would have resulted in our being deported immediately.

But he went out and got his own stories. He went to Faridpur with Tom. A Hindu lady, who had been shot through the neck and left for dead by the Pakistan soldiers, came seeking help. Sidney knew the suppression by the army in East Pakistan was not just directed against men fighting for freedom. Helpless women and children were also being annihilated.

While in Faridpur, he visited the army officer in charge. He expressed himself openly to this officer. When he returned to his Dacca hotel, he was placed under surveillance and deported on the next flight out.

A few weeks later, a reporter from United Press International came to me. He opened his coat, and from an inside pocket he pulled out a map. He handed the map to me and said, "Sidney Schaneburg sent this from New Delhi." He continued, "He probably will not be able to return to East Pakistan since his last visit didn't go too well."

I had given Sidney the map indicating areas I though he should visit. The map could have been purchased anywhere in Dacca. But his returning it in this way made it valuable to me.

CHAPTER EIGHT

Was East Pakistan or "Bangladesh in Bondage" a place where a foreign family should live? We were continually asked this question. We also asked the same. But my family and the Thurmans answered it only for ourselves.

Two families in our mission had visas so they could return from regular furlough without any difficulty. Though we really wanted them to come, we chose not to make any recommendation concerning their return. It was impossible to describe the situation in East Pakistan responsibility at that time.

We were greatly relieved when Dr. J. D. Hughey of our Foreign Mission Board came to Dacca in early July. The decision making was now his. Dr. Hughey, for one week, ate every meal with the Thurmans and my family. We all slept at the Guest House. He had every opportunity to observe our families in the present situation.

Soon after his arrival he said, "I see no reason why the Bennetts and Teels cannot return." In his casual manner he continued, "Let's ask them to come." We all liked that. We wanted the Bennetts and Teels. His willingness for the Bennetts and Teels to bring their children gave us assurance. This told us, "This good man whom we respect so much thinks we are doing okay."

Nor was that week in July calm. One evening, just after darkness fell, we were eating on the back porch. A head-splitting explosion blasted our area of Dacca. Before the drinking glasses stopped rocking and the silver in the plates stopped rattling, Kathy said, "Dr. Hughey, you are still going to let the Bennetts and Teels come, aren't you?" As if nothing had happened, Dr. Hughey answered, "I think so, Kathy. You and the other children seem to do very well."

The explosion had taken place within a block of our house.

We were sure, though, that the Freedom Fighters had no intention of harming us.

A few nights later, we decided to eat at a restaurant four blocks from the Guest House even though we knew it was a little risky. Before we had even ordered our food, the building trembled from an explosion. Some people scrambled under the tables. But Tom Thurman ran out the door. We had left David, his youngest son, at the Guest House. Before others had settled down, Tom was back with David. After all the children had petted David a little, we ate our food in peace. If one could not accept this as part of life, he had no place in Dacca.

Dr. Hughey left. The same month Troy and Marjorie Bennett and their daughter, Debbie, came back to East Pakistan. My family's greatest benefit from their return was Debbie. She was a young teenager and a real boost to Cherie and Kathy. When school started in August, Marj taught Cherie along with Debbie since they were in the same grade.

Mrs. Wilkens, who had remained in Dacca with her husband through all of the civil war, taught Kathy. Betty taught Keith and Wade, so school progressed.

The Bennetts lived next door to the Guest House. One night in August they came over to watch a special television program on the little portable television which we had recently purchased. The Phil Parshalls also came.

President General Yahya Khan was to be interviewed by foreign reporters in Karachi, West Pakistan, on a live program. The adults and older children huddled closely to the little television. The smaller children were in the yard playing. The program began just before dark.

President Khan was still the belligerent General he had been on March 25th. He was also a good liar or else didn't know what was happening in "his" East Pakistan. His opening remarks centered around the "normal" situation in East Pakistan. According to him, his soldiers had everything under control. He also said that the trouble in East Pakistan had been created by a handful of people who wanted to destroy the nation.

In spite of his remarks, perspiration poured from his forehead as informed reporters asked deeply probing questions. Some viewers might have thought that it was just the television lights warming his face, but we knew better. Any child living in East Pakistan could have refuted his statements.

It was now dark. Betty quietly slipped out of the room to where the children were playing. A few minutes later several little feet, touching the floor lightly, entered the room. The yard was no place for any child at night.

Just as they entered, gunfire blasted out in what seemed every direction. The President rattled on, "Everything is normal in East Pakistan." We all fell to the floor.

I called out, "Let's get all doors closed so no one can enter the house." Some of us crawled to the doors, pulled them closed and locked them. It seemed like eternity. Phil Parshall said to Lindy, his little daughter, "Don't be afraid, it's just like a wild west show."

Tom Thurman, with Philip, his oldest son, slowly eased up on the steps thinking that they would be safer since bullets could enter in the door and strike them. But Tom was hardly seated when he came scrambling back down. He said, "Something shook this wall." The wall was brick and also ten inches thick.

Glass crumbled to pieces in a building just behind the Guest House. It seemed the firing was getting hotter. Tom called out, "Everything is normal."

Wade was having a tough time. I had him penned under my body with his face down. He twisted his freckled face around and with tears flowing down his cheeks, he said, "Daddy, let's go to America."

Fewer shots were now being heard. After a few minutes, all became deathly quiet. We carefully opened an outside door and looked out. Then, slowly, some of us went into the yard.

The para-military forces had a road block just outside our gate on the main road. We later learned that a group of Freedom Fighters had suddenly run upon the road block and didn't have time to turn back. This had started the short-lived battle. The news we heard was that the Freedom Fighters had been killed. A few days later, however, we heard on the Free Bangladesh radio station a young man say, "I am one who was supposedly killed a few nights ago on Mirpur Road."

Three young men were hiding just inside the wall of our yard. They were not armed, at least when Troy and I talked with them. I said, "Please, as soon as there is opportunity, climb over the wall and slip away." They agreed when I said, "The military may come inside the yard at any moment; then all of us will be in real trouble."

On the opposite side of the road, policemen crouched down with rifles drawn. Others stood behind trees ready to fire less than fifteen feet from the house. Still others stooped low against the wall separating our house from the road.

Television was no longer interesting. As soon as it appeared relatively safe, the Parshalls drove out the gate toward home. The Bennetts went to their house next door. The Thurmans and my family prepared for bed. After Keith and Wade were in the bed, I slipped outside. The men with rifles were still hovering near the ground just outside the yard wall. I went back in and put the boys on the floor where it seemed safer.

The next morning there were a few bullet marks on the house. One chip of brick had been blasted out near where Tom had been sitting. No wonder the wall shook the previous night. One bullet entered the upstairs through a three inch thick window facing.

The number of roadblocks in the city grew. This was an effort to uncover arms and explosives. It didn't succeed, for the number of explosions increased.

Large areas of the city were blocked off; and house to house searches were made for arms, explosives, and for those who appeared to be Freedom Fighters. This task must have been unsurmountable, for some who worked in government offices were Freedom Fighters on their off time. Most of the population willingly offered refuge for Freedom Fighters.

Usually foreigners' cars were not searched in Dacca. But when I went to Comilla and Feni, it was unusual if my car was not searched. Sometimes even my briefcase was checked. Dacca was the "Show Case." The number of the people in Dacca did increase in August, September and October. However this only made more confusion for the military roadblocks and searches.

One Saturday my family left Dacca early in the morning for Comilla. This was the first time Betty and the children had been out of the city for four months. I thought a visit with the Christians in Comilla would be good for them. It might also be an encouragement to our Christian friends. The Bengali food prepared by Mrs. Roy was perfect. The day had been most pleasant.

But near Dacca, just before night, we were caught at a river crossing with a caravan of military vehicles. I had been a fool. All of the good from the relaxing day was quickly depleted. This was a perfect place for an attack on the army by the Freedom Fighters. I did not have to tell the children this. They were aware of the danger.

After we had waited for an hour at the end of the line, a soldier motioned for us to move on the ferry. There was a small space left, but all of the remaining military vehicles were too large for it. That was my family's last trip outside of Dacca while it was East Pakistan.

I never felt safe when I traveled to Feni. Up to Comilla it didn't appear to be too dangerous. But the forty miles south of Comilla and the twenty miles east to Feni were quite different. But even the route up to Comilla was at times dangerous. About thirty miles from Dacca, mines were planted on the road. When an army vehicle hit the mine, the explosion shattered it to tiny pieces. The blast was so severe that a section of the road bed about thirty feet long and four feet high was scattered across the rice fields. Evidently one-tenth of that force would have put the vehicle out of action.

A short distance away, a public bus was lying across the road with the front end blasted away. It had hit a lesser mine.

Because I traveled this route regularly, I fully knew what to expect. Houses in this area were burned by the army. Bloated bodies of cows, slaughtered by the army, dotted the fields. And the outside world was reading about possible famine in East Pakistan. Inside, an army, in anger, was killing cattle and leaving them to rot for the vultures to devour more easily.

But I can fully assert, though I surely did not know how to understand it all, God was good. Often before I started to Feni, I reminded Betty of financial matters that would make it easier for her and the children in the event I did not return.

I avoided every possible break in the pavement up to Comilla. Until September, however, a large section of the remaining route was dirt or gravel. I rode lightly on this section of the road. I felt my face tighten and burn. After reaching Feni and also returning to Comilla, I massaged my face, for it felt like one hardened muscle.

Usually when I went to Feni, I spent the night in Comilla on the return trip. This gave me an early start for the four ferries en route to Dacca. There had always been three, but a fourth one had been added since the Freedom Fighters had destroyed one large bridge. Sometimes there were long delays at these crossings.

Even this situation didn't remain. One morning I arrived at Feni. Someone said to me, "You won't be able to return to Dacca. Three more bridges have been destroyed."

That day I visited with the local civil government officer, Mr. Akund. He was in the office previously occupied by Mr. Belal, the West Pakistani.

Mr. Akund said, "When are you returning to Dacca?" I replied, "I'm not sure. I understand three bridges near Dacca were destroyed last night." I had hardly gotten the words out when I realized my mistake. He quickly asked, "How is this? How do you know three bridges that far away were destroyed last night?"

And I could not even remember who had told me. I mumbled a reply, "Perhaps it's just another rumor. You know how many rumors there are in this situation." I didn't know whether or not I could trust Mr. Akund. He was a Bengali, but some Bengalis were collaborators. He made a few phone calls, and my fears grew.

After some time he said, "No one knows anything about the bridges, so maybe it was just a rumor." He added, "You should be careful though."

"Then when are you going to Dacca?" he asked. "I am leaving this afternoon. I will spend the night in Comilla and go on to Dacca early in the morning," I answered.

He politely asked, "May I accompany you?" "Oh, yes. I would be glad to have you as a traveling companion." I replied.

That afternoon we drove to Comilla. He saw where the hundreds of houses had been burned but made few comments. Just before we reached Comilla, I asked him, "Where will you spend the night?" He slowly answered, "I have been thinking about that. I don't want to stay near any military people, so that doesn't leave many alternatives."

"Why don't you stay with me?" I asked. I was pleasantly surprised when he answered, "Oh, that would be very good, may I?" Ordinarily, a government officer of this rank would not have any difficulty in finding a comfortable place to spend the night.

I added, "I have no place to prepare food where I stay, but a Christian family prepares mine." Continuing, I said, "But I know they will consider it an honor to feed you also."

We reached Comilla. Mr. Akund said, "I will return in a short time." He returned before eating time and said, "You were right. Three bridges were destroyed last night. We won't be able to continue the journey by car."

He responded to the good food and gracious hospitality of the Roys. Soon it was dark; he and I climbed over the back fence to avoid the road and slept in the Buckleys' house.

Early the next morning we ate hurriedly and went to the bus stand. There were plenty of seats since only ten passengers were willing to be found on the road that day.

We reached the army base five miles west of Comilla. As usual there was a close check of all passengers on both the east and west side of the base. On the west side, after we had driven on the main road through the base, the military policeman was thorough. He closely observed the picture in my passport. The loss of twenty-two pounds following the tidal wave in 1970 had left my appearance a little different. But he was far more thorough in his checking of Mr. Akund. Several times I thought I should perhaps speak up and say that I was acquainted with him and that we were traveling together; but he was a government officer and should know how to manage.

After some time the policeman permitted our bus to proceed. I turned to Mr. Akund and said, "If you need my help at any time, please indicate it to me." Then I asked him, "Don't you have an identification?" He pulled his wallet out and showed me a documented identification. Then he said, "I absolutely refuse to show any identification to a West Pakistan foreigner. I am a Bengali. This is our country. Why should I prove who I am?" I no longer questioned his faithfulness to his people.

On the thirty mile trip from Comilla to the first ferry, we were stopped several times by the para-military personnel for a hurried check. At one such point, a young man stepped into the rear of the bus. He slammed the butt of his rifle on the wooden floor. The Bengali faces showed tenseness. I was sitting two seats in front of the door where the collaborator entered.

I turned and looked directly into his face with the severest look I could arrange. He couldn't take it. He melted. He lifted his rifle, did an awkward about face and stepped off the bus. There was complete silence. I am sure the Bengali passengers expected him to return with his companions and take me off the bus. I too, was a little nervous but did not regret what I had done.

After a slight pause, the young man struck the side of the bus with his hand indicating we could proceed. For about a minute no one said anything as we drove on. Then there was jubilation. One man rose from his seat, patted me on the back and then sat down without saying anything. Others called out. "Thank you, Sir. Thank you." Mr. Akund smiled. Though the U. S. government may not have been sympathetic to them, many Americans were. And for sure, most, if not all of the missionaries remaining in East Pakistan, continued to identify themselves clearly with the suffering Bengalis.

The destruction of those three bridges created new tensions. Our bus was stopped one-half mile from the ferry dock. We were told by the guard, "Only the military can enter this area."

The fields, due to monsoon rains, were covered with water.

We hired a small boat. Mr. Akund, Jason, who was a Christian young man from Comilla, and I crawled into the boat and continued our journey toward Dacca. We were cramped in the boat for six hours. The boatman and his son shared the food, which Sultan had prepared in Feni the previous day, with the three of us.

When we came within sight of each of the bridges, the boatman pointed them out to us. As we passed village areas, which were now little islands due to the heavy rainfall, some were left without a house. In other villages the people looked searchingly at us. We waved; they smiled and waved back as we continued. Friendship was sought by all.

On the last leg of the journey, Mr. Akund, Jason, and I climbed into a three-wheeled baby taxi with our luggage. We completely filled it.

At all the check points we were treated as suspects. At one of these I noticed that all of the para-military personnel were Bengalis. They were, no doubt, collaborators. On other occasions, I had pressed my "luck" so I decided to try it again. Before Mr. Akund or Jason got out of the baby taxi, I got out. I said to the would-be searchers, "You are Bengalis. Why do you search other Bengalis? This is their land as much as it is yours."

Their spokesman answered, "We are only doing our duty." I asked, "Is it your duty to be the enemy of your own people?"

I got back into the taxi and told the driver to proceed. I "cooled off" a little. Then Jason said, "Thanks, Mr. McKinley, but please be careful." Mr. Akund added, "These collaborators have no courage. Don't ever be afraid of them. But always watch them carefully. Don't press your luck too far."

I suppose I felt that through such actions I was defending the Bengali people. There were a few ways in which I could express my feeling toward the increasing brutality in Bangladesh. This was one way.

On the east side of the city Mr. Akund got down. We went on. Just as I entered the Guest House on the west side, the phone rang. "Did you make it okay?" said the voice on the other end of the line. "Yes, I made it okay," I answered. "Well, thanks for a very pleasant journey," came the reply. It was Mr. Akund.

A few days later, Pastor Simon Sircar of the Immanuel Baptist Church in Dacca said, "The next time you go to Comilla, I want to go with you." I reminded him of the danger in traveling as I did all those who asked to ride with me.

Pastor Sircar went with me to Comilla. I went on to Feni and returned to Comilla the following day. Comilla was without electricity again. It was reported that Freedom Fighters had destroyed a huge electric pylon a short distance north of the army base. That was too much to believe.

As we started back to Dacca, Pastor Sircar said, "Let's go see what happened." I replied that we might have difficulty turning north at the army base. Surprisingly, however, we were able to turn north, but on the northern side of the base, we were stopped by a military policeman.

He must have asked where we were going, but I didn't understand any of his Urdu. I spoke rapidly in English, "We are going a short distance north and will return in a few minutes." He again had not understood. But we drove on, and there it was. A vast steel structure had been toppled across the road. Burned electric lines lay tangled.

Pastor Sircar said, "Then we can believe most of what we are hearing. The courage of our Freedom Fighters is growing."

We turned and drove toward Dacca. At the first ferry I got out to pay the toll. I received our ticket from the Bengali ticket-collector. Then I started to walk toward our vehicle where Pastor Sircar was waiting. A soldier suddenly grabbed me by the hand. With his other hand he reached for the money in my shirt pocket. With all the strength I had, I pulled to free myself while he struggled to get the money. He was holding on to me with only one hand since his gun was in the other; so I was able to pull away. I couldn't believe what was happening. To rob a foreigner in daylight in the presence of others was being rather bold.

In fear, I screamed out in Bengali, "You may use your gun on me but I will not give you anything." Bengalis standing nearby moved away. Other soldiers, standing at some distance from us, came running and pulled him away. I asked, "If you do this to me, a foreigner, what are you doing to the Bengalis?" One of the other soldiers asked me to pardon my would-be robber. Without saying anything, I walked away and climbed into the vehicle.

I sat there trembling. Pastor Sircar said, "I am very much afraid, but thank you for what you did. You are trying to help us." I thought — if this is all I can do, I am not doing much. The incident seemed foolish. For a small amount of money, I ran the risk of real difficulty.

As we proceeded toward Dacca, my mind remained on the

river bank. The young soldier had been taught to be brutal. He was many miles away from home. Though he was in Pakistan and he was a Pakistani, he, no doubt, hated the Bengalis. This hatred had driven him and others to the point of being savage.

The nerve to try to rob a foreigner in a public place indicated the degree to which some soldiers had gone in their behavior. And they were treating Bengalis like the lowest form of animals. Also, it appeared to me that the governments of the world did not care.

India was speaking out. But her concern was self-interest. She had almost ten million Bengali refugees, and she had to rid herself of them. Then, too, any weakening of Pakistan gave her strength.

Big "brave" China was vocally supporting the Pakistani military government.

Russia did "lip-service."

But my deepest concern was the United States Government. American reporters, Congressmen and other citizens were voicing indignation at what was happening to the Bengalis. But if the U. S. Government cared at all, this care was never indicated.

If the United Nations is of any value to suffering people, Russia and the United States could have at least asked in this world forum — "Why is it that almost ten million people have fled their homes with tales of horror?"

I did not accept what was happening in East Pakistan as an internal matter. But I had no choice, it seemed, but to admit that there was little I could do about it. Not being able to do anything about such a tragedy created a deep inward struggle. There seemed to be a continual gnawing in my conscience.

Further help came to my family when the Howard Teels returned to East Pakistan from furlough. Their daughter, Marsha, provided more companionship for Cherie and Kathy. Their son, Stephen, was a boost to Wade and Keith.

But soon after their arrival, news came about problems relating to the schooling of two other daughters in Bangkok, Thailand. Mrs. Teel and the two children departed — never to return to Bangladesh.

I knew my children suffered from their going because of a remark Cherie made. She said, "It looks as if the older children could manage for themselves." She was really saying — we need Marsha and Stephen with us.

Every time something like this happened, I found myself examining the decision to keep my family in East Pakistan.

CHAPTER NINE

The East Pakistan Police informed me in early August that I should not travel to Feni any more. The reason given was that since Feni was a border town and becoming more dangerous, something might happen to me and they did not want to be responsible.

I was told that I could travel through Feni, however, if I were going south and Feni was not my destination. But the road south of Feni was one on which no one traveled due to its proximity to the border. I didn't have any reason for going further south, so I accepted this limitation.

I felt "tied down." This was not a new experience for me since in the 1965 India-Pakistan War, the Security Police had given me the same directive concerning Feni. Though my family had been evacuated from East Pakistan at that time, I had remained and lived in Dacca.

In 1965 I tried every possible way to get permission to visit our home in Feni. That permission came three months after the war ended. During that time I stayed with Pat Johnson, one of our missionaries in Dacca. One night Pat awakened me. He said, "You are sick. You were screaming." I answered, "Pat, I am not sick. I just want to go home."

The next morning I told Pat the full story. "Pat," I said, "I was only dreaming. And the best I can reconstruct the dream is that I was tied down on a table and hardly able to move. Several men, seemingly sympathetic, were standing nearby saying, 'You must not go.' I suppose those men were Security Officers telling me that it was not safe for me to go to my home in Feni." In 1971, I had no such dreams. But my desire to return home was just as great as it had been in 1965.

But I had a further problem with this restriction. If the restriction were placed on me by a West Pakistani, then I could easily accept it. This would have been further proof to me that someone other than an occasional West Pakistani Army Officer knew of my desire to aid suffering Bengalis and was determined to stop me.

However it seemed that this restriction was made by a Bengali Officer. To me, any intelligent government person knew that missionaries cared much for the suffering Bengali people; and he also knew that missionaries are not servants of any foreign government. So even though there might be danger to me, why would a Bengali place any restriction on me? I usually, during this time, found myself relating everything to the total effort for Bengali freedom. So I associated any action against me as being against the Freedom Movement in East Pakistan.

I could not accept that those in authority at that time cared about the safety of missionaries. Three missionaries had been killed. And two of those had been killed by West Pakistani soldiers. Not even one missionary had been deported. The only reason why government at that time might care about the safety of missionaries was that it could bring some embarrassment to the government if too many of them were killed. Gradually the outside world might actually begin to think that law and order was beyond the control of the government and that some of the stories being told about what was happening were really true.

But all I could do was accept the restriction. I had no grounds for an appeal. I only hoped the restriction had come from a West Pakistani officer. Of course, I will never know from whom it came. Maybe I should have accepted this as a restriction placed not only on me but as a general restriction. At any rate, it did not seem right to me that other foreigners were living in our house and I could not go near it.

I did maintain some relationship with the few friends who were still living in the Feni area. One of the Christian young men, with whom I worked, met me regularly in Maijdi, the Noakhāli District headquarters town. Since Maijdi was some distance from the border, I was not restricted from visiting there.

On the other hand, I was well rewarded from every visit to Comilla-Noakhali area. The greatest thrill came in August before the restriction was placed on me.

I was not able to travel by my vehicle since so many bridges had been destroyed, so Troy Bennett, one of my missionary companions, took me as far as his vehicle was permitted to go. We arrived at a large river. A ferry was waiting. I quickly got out of Troy's vehicle, and he turned back toward Dacca. I walked down to the ferry only to discover that it was for military personnel only. The Pakistan army was on a campaign in this area and were holding the ferry for any necessary use.

An hour later, the army released the ferry; and a few Bengalis and I crossed the river. On the other side I searched for transportation; but since the campaign was on, only a few pedestrians were found. There was no choice but to walk.

My few traveling necessities were not too heavy at first; but I soon discovered that for a ten mile walk to the next river, they were too much. Two young Bengalis offered to help me. I gladly accepted their response. We reached the next river just before night. My two friends arranged for a small boat to take us across.

On the other side, the army had gathered for the night. One of the young men pathetically said, "Sir, don't leave us. We are very much afraid of the army. If they catch us after night, you know what will happen to us." I knew. But what could we do?

At night no public conveyance traveled the roads. I said, "Let's start walking and at least get out of this place." Even without these two new young friends, my conscience would not let me spend a night with army personnel. As we walked, we talked. One of the young men asked, "What are you going to do?" I answered, "Perhaps I can find a village where I can spend the night."

"Let's try to locate a cycle rickshaw," remarked one of my friends; "then we can go as far as possible." As we walked and watched for a rickshaw, he said, "Sir, if you will help us get past all of the military check-posts, we will find a place for you to spend the night." I gladly accepted his suggestion. We found a rickshaw which took us about three miles. It was now dark.

We offered another rickshaw driver a good sum of money, and he agreed to take us nine miles if I could arrange to get past the check-points. We started moving in the darkness. My friends sat back in the seat. I sat in the middle on the front portion. It was raining so we kept the top up. My friends were hidden from view of the para-military forces who were soon checking us. I told the rickshaw driver, "Leave everything to me. Please do not say anything."

We approached the first check-point. I was nervous, not for

myself, but for these two young men. The rickshaw driver slowed down. I pointed the ready flashlight into my white face. The guard quickly motioned for us to proceed. I said to the driver, "Faster! Faster! He might call us back; but if he does, keep going!" As soon as we were out of rifle range, we stopped. The young men laughed and said, "Will this work again? There are many checkpoints." I replied, "We will at least try it."

It seemed at every little bridge there were guards. But we only had to slow down. We were always motioned on when I shined the light in my face. Had this been the regular army doing the checking at night, we might not have been so successful. But these para-military personnel were collaborators who again had little or no courage.

But I do not try to write it off that easily. I found that God managed when there was total dependance on Him. And this seemed more true when I was trying to help others. My two new friends were now old friends.

We turned down a little dirt path. Then the road ended at a large body of water. One of my friends said, "I will take a boat and see if it is okay for you to stay in this village tonight." The village belonged to some of his distant relatives.

After a few moments the friend called out across the water, "It's okay. Come on!" The other friend and I got into a small boat and in a few minutes were entering the village.

An elderly Muslim gentleman with a long flowing beard greeted me. He said, "Yes, you may spend the night with us." It was now about 11:00 p.m.; I was tired, for I had been traveling about fifteen hours. Part of the time I had been nervous, and this had caused a greater drain of energy. But these kind village people were not ready for bed. They wanted to talk.

I told them about myself and then about my family and our last few months in Bangladesh. They asked many questions about Betty and the children. They seemed surprised but grateful that we had chosen to stay in their country at the time of their Freedom Struggle.

They served me rice and curry. I shared my fried chicken and bread with the children. I ate but didn't really feel hungry. This was my first food since breakfast that morning. Things other than eating had been more important.

At about midnight, the elderly gentleman showed me where

100

I would sleep. The bamboo house had only one room. The room was divided into two sections by a bamboo frame about six feet high. The men and boys slept in one side. The women and girls slept in the other.

I sat down on the only bed that I saw. It was a simple wooden frame with a clean piece of cloth over it. A cane mat was on the floor. Little boys lay down on it. Some of them were soon fast asleep. Others waited for the elderly gentleman to join them. Apparently some of the men slept in another little house.

The women in the other section of the room called the elderly gentleman. I listened carefully to the conversation. It was about me. Their voices indicated concern, maybe even fear as they asked, "Isn't it dangerous to keep this white man here tonight? What if the army comes?"

I listened even more carefully for his answer. "No," he replied, "if the army comes, he may be able to help us." If my presence meant a slight amount of security to these humble people, then I had been paid for the difficult journey.

But there was more. The women asked, "But what if the Freedom Fighters come?" There was a pause. I was not anxious but very much interested in his reply. "If the Freedom Fighters come," he said, "his presence will not mean any danger for us, because he is one of us."

I did not feel that I had cheated in listening. But I did feel as good as I had ever felt in my thirteen years in Bangladesh. So many times I had wanted to be accepted by the non-Christians, but it always seemed there were miles between us. But now, because of a civil war, I had been driven to this village. And his statement, "He is one of us," was enough reward for any amount of trouble.

The two young friends joined me on the wooden frame. The elderly village leader turned the little kerosene light down low. He joined the little boys on the mat. All of my companions were soon fast asleep.

But there was no sleep for me. The bed was impossible for my lean frame. My bones seemed to rub holes in the plank. But there was a sense in which I was glad I could not sleep. It was a night of reflection and contemplation.

My one month's salary would have built a much better house, with all of the furnishings, than the one in which I was sleeping. But I was being treated with the deepest respect. My family enjoyed a good house, good food, and sufficient clothing. While it was true that we, too, had recently known fear, ours did not compare with theirs. The army often moved in and burned every house in some villages. These people with whom I was sleeping knew of this possibility for them. I chose to think that my presence helped them to fall asleep more easily that night.

My reflections brought only one conclusion. God had been good to me. I loved the family He had given me. I was loved. What more could I ask for? But beyond this, could I not contemplate a better life? Could I not give more of myself? So much had been given to me.

The night at times seemed long, especially when I thought of the possible visit of military personnel to this village. I became cold. But there was nothing I could do about it except to pull my sweater more closely about me.

The light of a new day began to break. I glanced down to the floor. Six little boys and the elderly grandfather were beginning to stir. The little legs and arms were so entangled that they looked more like an octopus. The grandfather sat up, and then we all arose.

I sat on a log outside the house. There must have been twenty men and boys in this part of the village. We all talked freely. One of them said, "We just can't believe it. You spent the night with us, didn't you?" I answered, "Yes, I believe I did."

We ate popped rice and drank hot tea. The rice was dry, but the hot tea warmed my body.

Other village people joined us. There were many questions about my presence. Some thought I was a reporter. Others thought I was fighting with the Freedom Fighters against the army. I explained again who I was.

The elderly village leader said, "Last night you told us about your work, and you told us about your family. But we do not understand why you can stay in our country where there is so much killing and destruction. I know it must be your religion. Will you tell us something about it?"

He had said, "He is one of us." Now he, a devout Muslim gentleman, was asking me, a preacher missionary, to share my faith with him and his friends. I was again being over-paid for my previous day's journey.

I spoke personally and briefly of what Jesus meant to me. Everyone seemed to listen with interest except one man who spoke up and said, "We do not want to hear this." The elderly leader turned to him and said, "I asked this man to speak. We will hear what he has to say."

When I finished, there was silence. A few minutes later I expressed my thanks and stepped into a little boat to cross the body of water. I walked about a mile and found a three wheel baby-taxi waiting for a good fare. He had one in me.

As the vehicle bounced along the road toward Comilla, I saw smoke swirling into the sky some distance away. "Please slow down and watch carefully," I said to the driver. The taxi stopped. It was all over. Not one person was in sight. I estimated that a thousand little houses had been burned the previous night. Nothing was left but smoldering pieces of wood, some burned tin roofing and little earthen foundations of the houses.

My anger boiled. Somewhere, in other nearby villages, refugees from this area were trembling in fear. In a few days some of them can slip across the border into India, I thought. But all were now in agony.

I felt so helpless. I got back into the little taxi, and we drove on. Later I learned that it had been reported to the army that this area was the home of some young men who were Freedom Fighters. Mothers and children, elderly women and men, the lame, the blind were paying the price for freedom along with the strong, brave young Bengali men.

After a few days I returned to Dacca. The usual screams, "Mother! Daddy is back!" greeted me. Those screams sounded better each time.

Dacca city continued to shake at night as explosions ripped vital installations. These explosions reminded us that someday Bangladesh was to be free. The foreign adult community of Dacca gradually grew, but only a few children made their way back to Bangladesh. We carefully watched for the arrival of any children who might become a companion for one of ours.

The strength — emotional, physical and spiritual — of Cherie, Kathy, Keith, and Wade was an encouragement to Betty and me. The Christian home was more important than ever before to us. We thoroughly understood that family members need one another.

Birthdays for the year 1971 ended in August with Cherie's being thirteen, Kathy twelve, Keith seven and Wade five. Though they were occasionally afraid, concern for the Bengali people, especially the children, was always apparent. I felt they were well rooted in the soil of Bangladesh — or at least as much as "foreign" children could be rooted.

In September, Marjorie Bennett was teaching Cherie along with her daughter, Debbie. One of their lessons called for the writing of a poem. Betty and I noticed that Cherie had been laboring over something for several days. One day she brought to us, on her yellow school paper and written in pencil, this poem:

Roaring out of the Bengal sunset they came,
Two black dots on a warm summer evening.
Some children stop their playing to set clear
    eyes upon them,
In awe watching the pair, soaring over rice fields
    and straw huts
Like finches looking for some place to rest
    their wings.

But suddenly, as they spot the tiny town,
Their nature changes, and now, like vultures,
They screech and dip down upon it.
A piercing wail rings out and then,

    BOOM! . . . BOOM! . . . BOOM!

The children scatter like frightened ants
    into their houses,
Amid the constant shattering and blasts.
Flinging themselves upon the floor,
They lay frozen in fear,
Their faces ghastly, their blood cold, their
    heads buzzing with the question, "Why?"
While outside, the vultures peck at their prize.
A mother tries to comfort a child with shaking
    hands.
The only steady comforting sound is the thunk,
    thunk, thunk of the father's feet
Pacing the floor.
Again and again the planes dip,

    BOOM! . . . BOOM! . . . BOOM!

Then in the same mysterious way they appeared,
They are gone.

104

All is quiet, The world seems dead.
But . . . off in the distance comes the clattering
    of wheels on the old road,
And the jingling of bells.
Like water from a broken dam,
The living gush into the countryside,
Trying to escape from the smell of death and blood.
Some crying, some with faces of white stone,
They all plod along together.
Not saying a word,
Not having to, because their grief is written
    on their faces.
Slowly, they filter away.
The night comes, the stars twinkle,
A cool breeze blows from the south.
The only irritating sound is the crickets which
    seem to say . . .

    LOVE YOUR ENEMIES . . . LOVE YOUR ENEMIES . . .
        . . . . . LOVE YOUR ENEMIES.

Cherie had relived the day the jet planes of the Pakistan Air Force first struck Feni. It took me about thirty minutes to read the poem. Feeling was deep. But I thought she, with God's help, had come through beautifully in her struggle against hate, hate toward the Pakistani soldiers. My thirteen year old daughter understood love and forgiveness better than I, her missionary father. Hatred hounded me continually — hatred against military forces that were treating Bengali people as if they were lower than the lowest form of animals.

But Cherie's poem helped me to pray more earnestly for the strength to love and forgive men who were brutal in their behavior to others.

I think Cherie both shamed me and embarrassed me through her beautiful experience. But the help I received was worth that shame and embarrassment.

Often Cherie and our other children asked me about how the people who had been left after the terrible tidal wave of the previous year were doing. I had no way of telling them the facts since I had not visited their area since April. I decided that I should go to the tidal wave disaster area and see if I could help. How to travel I did not know. But I started in that direction.

It was now the middle of November. I was able to drive from Dacca to the Catholic Mission near Maijdi, the Noakhali District headquarters. As I drove along the inland road, there was evidence of a change in the military situation.

The city of Comilla was surrounded by a huge mound of earth, which I was told, was an anti-tank barrier. On the eastern and southern section of the army base, sharp pointed sticks, by the thousands, lined the side of the road and sections of the base area. Field guns, which I had not seen before, were being towed by trucks and jeeps.

Laksam, the railway center about fifteen miles south of Comilla, was surrounded by newly cut trenches and sharp pointed bamboo sticks. The road south of Laksam had been lined with small bunkers, but these were now abandoned. The Pakistan army was pulling its forces together for something bigger. From all appearances, they were preparing to meet another army — not small bands of Freedom Fighters.

I delayed only a short time at the Catholic Mission, for I wanted to reach the tidal wave disaster area before night. The Father in charge of the mission promised to try to protect the vehicle — so off I went in the little three-wheeled baby-taxi which had so often been my means of conveyance. The little taxi bounced like a rubber ball on the rough road. I held on tightly, but this did not prevent my head from banging the iron rods across the top of the little taxi.

The longer we drove, the worse the road became. Finally I told the driver, "Let me out. I will walk from here." The walk was pleasant and not too long. After about two miles, I reached a small river. The ocean tide was just beginning to make its way up the river channel. A few men sat on the river bank. One of them said, "A boat will come from the other side just as soon as enough water comes up the channel. It will probably take about two hours."

I sat down with the men, and we conversed in Bengali. Though I had been in this area sinking tube wells the previous year, I did not recognize any of the men; nor did any of them indicate that they recognized me. In fact, when I inquired, none of them had heard about the tube well project which had been completed about ten months earlier. They were also strangers to this locality.

But Char Alexander was only about ten miles beyond the river. I knew many people in that area. So I felt that if there were

Freedom Fighters nearby, I would certainly know some of them. I did not want to appear overly inquisitive, because it was apparent these men did not understand what I was doing in this remote area at such a time of civil war. But I asked, "Are there any Freedom Fighters around?" An elderly man asked, "Why? Do you fear them?" I replied, "Oh, no! I only thought I might know some of them since I know many young men whose homes are on the other side of the river."

There was a long pause. Then the elderly gentleman said, "Sir, we are all Freedom Fighters." The conversation became warmer. Sometimes it appeared they did not trust me; but when I asked about Mr. Azad, a nearby Union Council Chairman, their faces brightened. "We do not know where he is now, but we have heard many good reports about his courageous fighting against the Pakistan Army," one young man answered. "But we know he is now a Captain with the Freedom Fighters."

Mr. Azad had helped us many times when we were sinking tube wells and distributing blankets following the tidal wave. On one occasion we took three hundred blankets to his Union for distribution. The names of those to receive the blankets were called out over the loud speaker. Only four of the three hundred were absent. I was convinced that Mr. Azad was concerned for his people, for often the lists were jumbled and many people absent at the time of distribution. This meant we had to make an extra trip. Now he was leading them in their struggle for freedom.

While we were waiting for the tide to come in, two small boats jammed with people came up the deepest part of the channel. I asked, "Who are those people?" One man answered, "They are moving to another place seeking safety." He continued, "You know the Hindus are being blamed for the present Freedom Struggle; but, of course, most of these people know nothing of what it is all about except that the army is trying to kill them because they are Hindus." They were some of the most destitute people I had seen in the past few months.

Our boat arrived and took us across; but because of the sloping bank on the other side, we had to walk about three hundred feet through deep mud. After climbing out of the mud, the passengers scattered across the fields toward their homes. They walked rapidly since darkness was approaching. The tidal wave had taken a heavy toll in this area, but that was now history. We were involved in a much deeper crisis.

Some of these new friends helped me get a cycle rickshaw after we had walked for about three miles. I asked the rickshaw driver to do his best, for I wanted to make Char Alexander before complete darkness. My rickshaw pulled into Char Alexander with the darkness. There were only a few men in the large market area with dimly lighted lanterns and small lamps. The quietness was fearful. It was here that, eight months before, Mr. Alam, who was now the Foreign Secretary of the Bangladesh Government in exile, had led the five thousand men and boys out to meet the ship which they believed was loaded with Pakistani soldiers. We had also used a half-destroyed school building in this market as our office for sinking tube wells.

I met briefly with a few friends and then went with one of them, Mr. Nouman, to spend the night. I learned that the Union Council Chairman of Char Alexander who had helped us to distribute blankets was collaborating with the army. He was organizing the Razakars, para-military forces, in this part of the country. Of course, hatred against him was deep, and he no longer lived there.

The perplexing thing, however, was that a band of about twenty Razakars was living on top of a twenty-five feet high food storage building. By the time I arrived in the market, they had pulled the ladder up on top so that no one could climb up and attack them at night.

I asked Mr. Nouman about their presence in the market area. His reply was, "Up until a few weeks ago, they continually gave trouble to the local people. They took whatever they liked from us. Then when the Freedom Fighters learned of this, they came in one night and inflicted heavy losses on the Razakars. Since then they have lived to themselves." Mr. Nouman continued, "Actually, their presence here may now be considered fortunate for us. As long as they are here, the army will not feel a necessity for coming."

I had no comment to make. It was all confusing. Though the army did not feel the necessity for going to Char Alexander, they did go to nearby areas. They had burned houses and killed rural people as they chose. Some of the houses which were burned had been built following the tidal wave. I was continually "bugged" by the suffering about which I could do so little.

The next day, Mr. Nouman took me to see some lumber which we might buy to rebuild houses destroyed during the tidal waves. There was a Hindu village near the place where the lumber was

108

stored. A volleyball game was being played enthusiastically. Most of the men playing wore beards.

I asked Mr. Nouman, "If these men are Hindus, why are they all wearing beards?" He replied, "Some of them travel to make purchases; so a beard, which makes them look like Muslims, often helps them get past military check-points. Possibly their beards keep them alive." I was all for those beards if they helped in any way.

I told Mr. Nouman before I left, "Buy the lumber, if you can, and do all possible to help these suffering people. I will return as soon as there is opportunity and aid you further in the building of these houses."

The Razakars saw me several times but never inquired about my presence. As I left, I felt that they would not harm Mr. Nouman since they knew that any further disturbance would mean another raid by the Freedom Fighters who could easily defeat them. Public support for the Freedom Fighters made the difference.

The cross-country trip back to my vehicle at the Catholic Mission was slow as travel was in this troubled land. I spoke briefly with the Father in charge of the mission and then started toward Comilla.

As I traveled, I was more convinced that the Pakistan army was preparing to fight India. Bunkers had been more securely fixed. Tanks and field gun movements were common. But no one seemed to notice me as I drove along the road.

For every mile behind me I was grateful. I began to feel that I might be cut off from Betty and the children in Dacca. I stayed overnight in Comilla but without incident reached Dacca the next day.

And I heard for the last time the familiar screams, "Mother! Mother! Daddy is back!" from Kathy's shrill voice. This was my last trip in what was officially East Pakistan. On my next trip, there would be no fear for me from Betty and the children. I would be traveling in a free Bangladesh!

CHAPTER TEN

The city of Dacca became fearfully quiet. At night we heard only the roar from army vehicles. Though I had seen what appeared to be military preparation for an invasion from India on my last trip to Noakhali, I still chose to believe that India would not become directly involved in the fighting in East Pakistan.

A few days after my return to Dacca, word came that all of the ferry boats on the Dacca-Comilla route had been sunk by the Freedom Fighters. This partly explained the reason for the quietness in Dacca. Perhaps preparation was being made for the invasion. I had deep feelings about India's involvement, but my family was ready to welcome an invasion from the Bengali Freedom Fighters.

John Freeman, a missionary doctor in Thailand who had been a college friend of mine, wrote saying, "I am coming to visit you." I wrote back immediately, "No, don't come." John had wanted to visit Bangladesh ever since the tidal wave had struck the previous year. I wanted him to come, but not under the present circumstances.

The Thurmans came to Dacca to meet with the Bennetts, Howard Teel, Betty and me. Then too, Bill Marshall, who was the Area Representative of our Foreign Mission Board, arrived in late November. Bill had tried on several occasions to visit us during the year but for different reasons had been kept away.

We welcomed Bill, for we were able to share freely with him. Since all of us were together, we decided to have a Mission Meeting with Bill leading our worship time. Bill had come in from the outside. Perhaps he saw us as we were — physically tired, emotionally disturbed, and spiritually drained. During one of the worship periods Bill said, "Let's give the children an opportunity to share with us some of their feelings."

For a long time, no one spoke. Then Keith, who was now

111

seven, got up and walked across the room to Betty. He wanted to speak but wasn't sure he should. Betty told him to go ahead and speak if he wanted to say something. Then, in a broken, quivering voice, he went back to our experience in Feni almost eight months before by saying, "When we were lying in the hallway of our house in Feni while the planes were attacking, all I could think of was our poor Bengali friends who were being killed." Tears flooded his face and ours.

But through this experience, hope came again. This time it came through our little foreigner who loved his Bengali neighbors. Our children were not coming apart emotionally as some had predicted. Rather, life with depth was taking on new meaning for them.

I have always felt that in a mission organization, the lives of missionaries are more entangled than any other group. Everyone is very much involved in the life of others in the organization. This is both good and bad. When bad, someone gets hurt. Often the group feels that only group decisions are the answer.

An example of this was our decision as a mission in the 1965 India-Pakistan war. We voted that all women and children were to be evacuated. We then asked one man to accompany them.

When the war broke out on March 25, 1971, there was no opportunity for a meeting. But remembering the way we had handled the situation in 1965 had caused me to write to all of our missionaries in early March of 1971 that decisions concerning the difficulties should be made by each family and that all of us should support others in their decisions. I strongly believed this was right.

But in our meeting in late November when it now appeared that all-out war, involving India also, might possibly break out, I found myself presiding over a meeting discussing which ones of us should prepare to leave the country. It was obvious that if anyone were to leave, my family was to be considered first. Both we and the Thurmans had been present the entire time of the war. We had also been present at the time of the tidal wave and the strong relief program following. But my family was now in its fourth year in East Pakistan, so we were soon due a furlough. The discussion centered around the possibility of our leaving for early furlough.

Being the chairman of the group caused difficulty for me, but I was eventually able to lead our missionaries away from that discussion. I believed then and still believe that in time of war, I should not say what others should do; nor do I believe others should say what my family should do. This could be a life or death matter —

hence each family should be free to decide for themselves what they will do.

But we had gone too far. Cherie, Debbie and Kathy had been in the meeting when we had discussed the possibility of my family's leaving East Pakistan. A few days later this caused real difficulty for us.

Foreign news broadcasts revealed that heavy fighting was taking place on all the borders of what was still East Pakistan. Still fewer people were seen in the streets of Dacca.

We put down a well at the Guest House in the event our water supply should be cut off. We bought kerosene for the lanterns and wood for cooking fuel. First-aid supplies and medicines were gathered, and at least a two week's supply of food was brought in. Though the prices were exorbitant, we especially bought tin-canned food which could be easily prepared. Now as I look back over it, little did we understand that for which we were preparing; but we were fully sincere in everything we did. We thought we were prepared for the worst.

John Freeman cabled that he was arriving. Apparently he had not received my letter. I met him at the airport. He had received my letter but felt he might be needed.

Bill Marshall had a meeting scheduled in India, but he said, "I'm not needed there; I'll stay here with you folks."

Though we wanted him with us, we encouraged him to go. His family was thousands of miles away at their home in Nicosia, Cyprus. Still nothing was happening in the Dacca area, so Bill decided to go. The late afternoon of December 2nd, he flew Pakistan International Airlines to Karachi, West Pakistan. We did not know it then, of course, but Bill made a historic flight. That was the last regularly scheduled passenger flight ever to depart East Pakistan.

At bedtime that night all was calm. The Bennetts' house was less than twenty-five feet away from the Guest House. The Thurmans, Howard Teel and John Freeman were upstairs in the Guest House. We were downstairs. Cherie and Kathy's bedroom was across the hallway from Betty's and my bedroom. Keith and Wade's room was next to the one in which Betty and I slept. We prayed with the children as usual and went to bed.

Sometime past midnight, now December 3rd, "hell" broke loose in the city. The entire area was suddenly filled with ear-splitting blasts. I ran to get Cherie and Kathy while Betty was bringing the boys into our room. Then I said, "Don't be afraid; it's the

Freedom Fighters attacking the army. You know they won't hurt us."

There was a brief calm. Then, suddenly, it sounded as if the city were being taken apart. Betty said, "Listen, there is a siren." We heard the roar of jet engines. It was now apparent that it was not the Freedom Fighters but the Indian Air Force. In a few minutes time, it seemed that the planes filled the sky over Dacca. They were making an all-out attack on Pakistan military installations.

We pulled the foam rubber mattresses off the beds and dragged them into the narrow hallway of the Guest House. The Thurmans were there almost by the time we were. All of our careful preparation seemed meager. We needed a bomb shelter. But we did our best by holding the foam mattresses over our heads since we expected the ceiling plaster to fall. Howard and John joined us, but they did not have the anxiety of those of us with children. In a mess like this, any rational man had to ask himself — have I played the part of a fool? What right does any man have to keep his family in a country that had already been at war for more than eight months? We and the Thurmans knew well what spewing bullets from jet fighters could do. No one doubted that bombs and rockets do more. The small children cried. We parents tried to remain steady. It wasn't easy. Tom suggested that we sing. We were not able to compete with the outside noise, but singing did help. "Jesus loves the little children, all the children of the world," rang out. Then, "Jesus loves me, this I know . . ." and also, "Holy, Holy, Holy, Lord God Almighty." But the singing didn't last long.

Then Betty said, "Let's think about all of our friends who are praying for us." The grandmothers and grandfathers, uncles, aunts, and cousins were praying. They knew of the danger we were in before Dacca was attacked, for we shared freely with them through our letters. Missionary children primarily know their grandparents through the stories their parents have told them. They, because of this, know they are loved. Now they had been reminded of that love. This helped greatly.

But we also talked about others around the world who were praying for us. Included among those were missionary friends from many countries. Many of them, too, well understood the danger in war. Bill Marshall was among those missionary friends. He was now getting a close look at the same war over on the other side of India in West Pakistan.

Then there were missionary friends from Great Britian, Australia, and New Zealand who had previously served in East Pakistan. They knew the situation well. We remembered them, knowing they remembered us.

Also there were the churches from which we had come. They claimed us as their own in Christ. In many countries, especially in Asia, we had Christian friends other than the missionaries. Many of them had seen more of war than missionaries ever experience. Their prayers had real strength.

In Thailand, Baptist missionaries would be praying because one of their own, John Freeman, was with us and because Howard Teel's family was there.

Separated from both Mom and Dad were Steve and Becky Bennett. Steve was at Mars Hill College in North Carolina, and Becky was in Bangkok. Surely their prayers for Mom and Dad would spill over on us next door.

But perhaps the greatest help came to the children when someone mentioned Dr. Hughey. Dr. J. D. Hughey was our "Boss", but the children knew him as a dear friend. He had been with us for almost a week in July. That visit, done without hurry, had lifted our two families when we were rather low. The children had nothing but pleasant memories of him.

We didn't know it then, but back in Richmond, Virginia, Dr. Hughey was having trouble of his own. He was the one whose responsibility it was to initiate any action by our Foreign Mission Board concerning our departing this war-torn land.

Later when Dr. Hughey told us of his struggle as to whether or not he should ask us to leave East Pakistan, we loved him even more. He said, "I felt, though it wasn't easy, that you knew the situation. I left the decision to you." This man of God proved to us his respect, his love, and his faithfulness; but, most of all, he showed his faith in the missionaries God placed under his administrative responsibility. We knew, though, that Dr. Hughey did not leave all of the praying to us. He was praying, too; and he was calling upon others to pray for us.

So what could happen to missionary families in such a situation? Well, they could get killed; but with such faithful prayer support, surely they could take it well if that time came.

In the Guest House hallway, the tension eased a little. A few smiles could be seen as the small flashlight at times carefully provided the needed light. All became quiet again. We went back

115

to our rooms expecting to sleep. But in a few minutes, we charged back into the hallway, for again it seemed better protected. Planes again filled the skies of Dacca. Bombs and rockets burst. Anti-aircraft guns blasted away at those attacking planes.

Dawn of December 3rd caught us still in the hallway. We tried to eat breakfast on the porch in a normal way but found that impossible. We couldn't swallow well with planes swooping over our heads. The attacks continued throughout the day. There was less fear, however, since we could see the planes in action, and we knew their targets were military.

But the day-time revealed more clearly the night-time danger. The military targets were clearly seen in the day-light. At night, those targets were hidden by darkness. Darkness may have been the reason for a children's home being blasted by bombs one night. Huge craters, splintered buildings and mangled bodies of little children caused us to think of what might happen to others and to us.

As the crow flies, the Guest House was slightly more than one mile from the end of the airport runway. We had a clear view of the fighting. On December 4th, each attack by the Indian planes brought the jet fighters of the Pakistan Air Force into the sky. The pilots of these older and slower planes strongly challenged the sleek fast jets of India. Aiding the Pakistan planes were the shells of the anti-aircraft guns which hammered away at the attacking Indian planes. The bursts of those shells filled the sky with huge pockets of white smoke.

We saw planes explode in the air and crash to the earth. Others, burning furiously, crashed with an earth-shaking thud and sent up a cloud of black smoke.

Shrapnel filled the yards of residences in the airport area. Some of the pieces were small, but others were large enough to crush in the top of some automobiles. We usually stood under the carport or ledge of the house when we watched.

The smaller children had no desire to watch. They were too fearful. Cherie and Wade especially wanted me to stay under the mattress covered tables even during the daytime for fear that I might be hurt. They, along with Keith and Kathy, had had enough experience with planes in Feni to last them a life-time. Seemingly, however, Keith and Kathy did not have quite so much fear as did the others.

Early that morning a representative of the American con-

116

sulate came to the Guest House. His message was, "All Americans desiring to leave are to come to the Intercontinental Hotel this afternoon with one suitcase each."

Betty said without consulting me, "Please put the children and me on the list. We will be leaving." I was stunned. I had no idea she would decide so quickly and so convincingly. I remembered our discussion a few days earlier in the Mission Meeting when it had been said that if anyone should leave, it should be the McKinleys. Our furlough time was approaching.

But I was silent. Betty didn't ask me how I felt. She knew this. Since the final word had not been given on the arrival of the evacuation planes, they stayed at "home" that night.

The next day the message came again, "The planes will arrive tomorrow. Either come to the hotel this afternoon or early in the morning." But since our house was only about one-half mile from the hotel, Betty and the children prepared to stay at "home" another night.

Betty shared her decision with the Thurmans, and I went next door to tell the Bennetts.

Betty knew that I didn't want them to leave. I couldn't ask them to stay after they seemingly felt that they must go, because for eight months even the sound of planes had caused our faces to redden with anger and our spines to tingle.

We went to bed the night of December 5th, thinking that was our last night together as a family, perhaps for a long time. It was one of my most miserable nights of the more than eight months of war. If it is a weakness for a man to want to be with his family, then my weakness sprang forth vividly.

As I tossed and wiped away tears and tried to pray, I thought only of the good I had enjoyed with Betty and the children during those past eight months. We had grown together as a family, but now we were going to be "taken apart". I was fearful of this. The land of East Pakistan had left its mark on us.

I especially thought about our children. I recalled how little Cherie had learned to walk and talk with Bengali children after her arrival in East Pakistan when she was ten months old. The Bengali language, in her early years, was as much a part of her as was English.

This was also the case for Keith and Kathy, our true children of the soil; for they had been born in the land of the Bengalis.

117

Though the evacuation of my family during the 1965 India-Pakistan War had been responsible for Wade's having been born in the Philippines, he, too, had to be considered "one of the Bengalis" for he had arrived in East Pakistan by the time he was three weeks old. Yes, regardless of the future situation, the Bengali people and their country had our children's love forever.

I, too, knew that Betty loved the Bengalis. She didn't want to leave, but our discussions had indicated that she should go. God had not simply called me to this land. He had also called her; and as best we understood, that call continued.

But in the midst of these circumstances, how could I expect her to remain? As far as we knew, she and Gloria Thurman were the only two foreign women whose children had been in the midst of the chaos for the entire time. If any mother with her children had a "right" to leave, Betty shared that "right" with Gloria.

The morning of December 6th was a gloomy one for my family. We had little to say as we shared breakfast. The suitcases were ready, and I prepared to take them to the hotel where all those to be evacuated were gathering.

The more I thought about being separated from them, the more I dreaded it. Then, in a moment of weakness, I said to Betty, "Why don't you stay?" Her answer was ready, but even still she paused briefly before saying, "Let me talk with Cherie and see what she says."

Betty and Cherie went into one of the bedrooms, closing the door behind them. One thing was sure — Betty did not want me to influence Cherie with any arguments of mine. She wanted her to be as free as is possible in such a situation to decide for herself.

But why Cherie? She was the oldest. She fully understood what had been happening to young Bengali women. The experience with the Pakistani planes in Feni had greatly troubled her. Her poem proved this. Now it wasn't just a few Pakistani soldiers, but a city filled with them surrounded by their enemy.

The previous two nights, Cherie and Betty had deeply felt the physical danger as the planes attacked. Kathy still did not seem to mind.

It seemed that Betty and Cherie were in the bedroom for a long time. The longer they remained, the more I feared their decision. Naturally I felt that a thirteen-year-old girl would not choose to remain in such a dangerous place if she had an opportunity to leave.

118

The door opened slowly, and Cherie came out first. Betty was leaving it to her to share with me. Her long blond hair flowed down almost to her waist. Tears streamed down her red cheeks. Betty followed closely. Cherie looked at me, but she couldn't smile. This matter of so much killing had taken its toll on her. She sobbed and with the back of her hand wiped away some of the tears. Then, in a broken voice, she said, "Daddy . . . Mother and I have talked. We have decided." She had trouble getting the words together. Then, with even greater difficulty, she said, "Mother and I have decided that we want to stay with you."

The salty water gushed down my face. Though I had never been more happy about my family, I had never wept more. God had kept us together again. Betty had made the right decision by letting Cherie decide fully for herself without any interference from me. But still she had not made the decision thinking only of herself. Her dad had figured strongly in it. Perhaps she didn't trust him alone. She knew he needed her Mother and her. And that, too, was okay by me. I did need them!

Cherie had many Bengali friends. Of course, she did not want to leave them. Debbie Bennett was three months old when Cherie arrived in East Pakistan the first time. They had shared many good days together. Cherie did not want to leave Debbie. During the previous eight months, Cherie had Kathy with her; but Debbie's sister Becky was in boarding school in Bangkok.

But even still, I knew I figured mainly in her decision for remaining. She and Betty knew that I had done many "foolish" things in traveling on mined roads and through areas that were involved in the actual fighting. I felt that they both knew their presence was vital in keeping me near the Guest House rather than out in a more dangerous area with others.

So this put me in a more difficult position. I had asked them to remain. If anything happened to them or to any member of the family, I was really in trouble. This led me to ask them, "If anything happens to any of us, please help me; for even now I feel that if I knew either of you failed to support me in such a matter, I would not be able to bear it."

Of course, I didn't expect them to reply to such a question or request. Surely we would all be all right.

I again became more concerned about physical provisions; so after sharing our news again with the Thurmans and the Bennetts, I went out to purchase more supplies.

Kathy watched for me while I was inside a little store buying more canned food. The store was north of the Guest House, so we were only a short distance from the airport while I did the shopping. The attacking planes, we were sure, were only after the airport. The days before us looked bleak, indeed. These days, we thought, included Christmas. It was proper, at least, to have food to eat at Christmas.

The evacuation didn't take place on December 6th as planned. Planes came, but reportedly they were fired upon by either the Indian Air Force or the Pakistanis.

The more the evacuation was talked, the more confused it seemed. I was glad Betty and our children were no longer involved in the process of waiting at the hotel and going through the distress. We had passed over the emotional strain of that decision. It now seemed to me that it was safer at the Guest House than trying to make the occasional run to the airport which each time was ending in disappointment for those who hoped to be evacuated.

As I watched mothers with children sob as they made several attempts to get to the airport, I was thankful that things had worked out well enough for us to be able to remain in Dacca.

It was reported that planes actually did come into East Pakistan territory a second time but had to turn back because of the fighting over Dacca between the planes of India and Pakistan. But Pakistan was losing the air battle. The planes were outdated and outnumbered; so, after a few days, India controlled the sky over Dacca.

But before this happened, we saw many of the ravages of war as planes tumbled from the heavens. The Pakistani pilots did not give up without a fight. As their planes went down, more Indian planes also crashed to the earth.

Some of us witnessed an Indian jet fighter going in for a dive over the airport. The plane came out of the dive and like lightning shot upward. But as it went, shells from the anti-aircraft guns hit their target. The plane became a ball of smoke and suddenly changed directions. A few seconds before the burning plane hit the earth, the pilot ejected and shot upward. His parachute opened, and he drifted slowly downward. That night the pilot was "displayed" on television in Dacca. His country may have been winning the war, but he had lost.

The airport was north of the Guest House, and further north was the army base. The Indian planes constantly pounded the base.

During the daytime we could see the bombers. We could see the smoke rise up and feel the "thuds" as the bombs struck, leaving huge craters. But they seemed far away from us when we could see it happening. At night those same "thuds" caused the Guest House to tremble and the doors and window shutters to rattle.

The delay in the evacuation helped us one way. An American, who was a friend of ours, had a large supply of food. He never expected to return regardless of the outcome of the war. In fact, he had more than our combined supply; so we were really glad when he said, "If you can use the food and are willing to take the risk of bringing it here, go get it and you can pay for it someday."

Because the other men were busy, my brave little Kathy said, "Daddy, I will go with you to get the food." In a short time we were on our way. We zoomed past the airport, but Kathy had her head out the window searching the sky for Indian planes which might attack.

Our friend showed me the store room. The food looked worth the risk we were taking to get it. I told Kathy, "While I load the food, you watch for planes. Let me know if you feel we should both take cover." I charged in and out of the house with arm loads of food while Kathy watched the skies. Planes appeared; and Kathy called out, "They are coming, Daddy, but keep on working." Then she said, "Sometimes they come pretty close, but I can tell they are after the airport."

Within an hour's time, there were several attacks on the airport; but we had our food in the vehicle. Now we were ready to make the run back to the Guest House. But, how to get back? That was the question. I flashed a smile at Kathy and said, "Are you ready?" She quickly answered, "No, I'm not ready" to go near that airport." She had seen too much in the last hour.

I couldn't fail a friend like Kathy. We had the needed food, and we had to get back to the Guest House quickly; for Betty and the others would be worried about us. But how were we to get back?

"Kathy," I said, "I know there is another road, but I have never traveled it. And we might run into the army; because, I understand, it runs through a rather desolate area of the city. What do you think?"

"Let's try it, Daddy," came the quick reply; "I think we can make it." So we roared down the unknown road. We had to make several turns, each time hoping they were the right ones. Soldiers were all over the area. They only glanced at us so we kept going. Kathy occasionally stuck her head out the window to look in the direction of the airport.

Once she saw planes; but the attack was a short one, so we kept moving. A little while later we were back on the airport road but at least one-half mile south of the airport. We continued moving rapidly south and finally a short distance west to the Guest House. Keith had the gate open. He called out as we drove into the yard, "Did you get it?" Kathy smiled as if she were the bravest and said, "Sure, why do you think we went?" We took part of the food over to the Bennetts next door. "Now, we're really prepared," we thought.

CHAPTER ELEVEN

We knew there was no preparation we could make to help in the event of a direct hit by a bomb. But we also knew something could be done to help if a bomb fell nearby or if there was street fighting in our area.

So John Freeman assumed the responsibility for preparing the Guest House as best he could. We helped John line the outside of the back porch with anything and everything we could find. We placed the refrigerator, the deep freeze, book shelves loaded with books, and every available piece of furniture in the place we felt it offered the most protection. We also prepared for blackouts by covering the windows and vents with heavy black paper. We removed the ceiling lights and all picture frames from the walls, for we didn't want anyone to be cut by glass.

The only things left in the room where we slept were the dining tables, a desk and the foam mattresses. At night we separated the narrow dining tables and placed them along the wall which appeared the safest. Kathy didn't want to be disturbed by any of us, so she chose to sleep under the desk. We covered the tables with the mattresses, and Cherie slept under the one nearest Kathy. Betty and Wade slept together near Kathy; Keith and I slept nearest the outside door.

The Thurmans moved downstairs and prepared their room by lining the outside wall with wooden closets. They moved a large chest near the table under which they slept. John and Howard moved into the Bennetts' house and prepared a room for themselves.

Pastor Sircar came asking to move in with us since their house was even nearer the airport and there were no friends nearby; for most people had vacated that area. His family was welcomed, of course.

The evacuation continued to be delayed and this created further havoc for those preparing to leave. In some respects, it didn't help us either. One foreigner came bursting into the Guest House one day and screamed out, "You had better leave. When the Bengali fighters come into this city, they will slaughter everyone left!"

I wondered what Cherie thought when she heard him. I knew his words were spoken without love for or an understanding of the Bengalis' situation. But Cherie had just gone through the difficult struggle of deciding whether or not to leave. And she knew that there were some Bengalis who knew nothing about our position and our relationship to other Bengalis. She also knew there were some who had learned to kill without thinking. They would not care what our position might have been.

But Cherie's decision had not been made lightly. Many times she had considered all of this and more, too. Her reaction was anger at this gentleman for his loose talk. The statement was too inclusive for a thinking Christian young lady, so she gave little attention to what he said.

The size of our group grew rapidly. Another pastor moved into a small brick building near the Bennetts' house with his family. Since one of the Bennetts' helpers already had his family there, they soon had their area filled. One large Christian family moved into the brick building in the Guest House area. They brought all of their precious belongings as did the other families, for they knew their houses would be looted.

The guards who worked for us at night began staying full-time since they might get caught by a sudden curfew. But they also remained because they felt safer with us. It wasn't long until they had a room filled with Bengali men.

The curfew, which sometimes lasted up to forty-eight hours, created real problems. The military order was to shoot on sight anyone breaking the curfew. This worked well for them. They were able to detect the movement of Bengali men easily. The slightest noise during a curfew created tenseness.

For us it primarily meant being extremely careful when we had to go outside, for military vehicles constantly passed by the Guest House. We occasionally had to go out for water, and at night we carefully checked the outside of the house to make sure no light was seen. The checking was done in complete silence.

When we opened the door to go out and to enter, we turned off the lights to make sure there was no shooting in our direction.

One afternoon the curfew was suddenly put into force. The service station next door was open, so the men quickly closed the doors and ran to their houses. But in haste they left all of the lights on.

Just as darkness fell, I looked out the back door. The bright lights from the service station glowed over the area. This made the station and our two houses a perfect target for the shooting planes.

I called out, "Keith, come, let's see if we can get those lights out." Those who heard us knew there was no other choice. The only word was, "Be careful." We ran out the gate; and as we reached the service station, a truck load of soldiers drove up. They jumped out with their guns ready. Apparently Keith and I didn't look too dangerous.

But the situation was a little tense. They were angry, so I said, "Sir, I'll turn the lights out somehow. Just give me a minute." I threw a brick through the glass door and entered. The soldiers still had their guns drawn. They seemed to think it was a plot, but I felt it was only a mistake. I found several light switches but couldn't find the main switch, so I shoved tables under the lights that I couldn't turn off, jumped up quickly and took out the fluorescent tubes. Keith stood nearby and held the tubes.

There was only one outside light left. After several throws with brick pieces, it crushed and the job was complete. Keith and I carried the light tubes to the Guest House. The soldiers said nothing as we left. A few minutes later, we heard the truck drive away. I am sure they scratched their heads trying to figure out who we were.

Perhaps they didn't know what we knew. The owner of that station was in prison on the military base. He had been arrested a few years earlier and accused by Pakistan of being a spy trying to overthrow the government along with Sheik Mujibur Rahman, who, as far as we knew, was still in prison in West Pakistan.

The next day during a short curfew break, I returned the tubes and told them I was the culprit who had broken their glass. No thanks were necessary, but they did thank me for helping them.

Someday I hoped to meet Mr. Rahman, the owner of the service station. From the accounts I had read of the trial involving the supposed conspiracy, one of the men had stayed in a small

125

hotel in Feni before crossing into India in their attempt to over-throw the government. That hotel was next door to our library in Feni. But that hope wasn't too strong; because from what we were hearing, no one would survive that military prison.

Tom Thurman's unassuming comics continued to bring laughs, but John Munshi gave him a challenge. John had been a friend of all of us for several years, but I had missed his funny side.

John lived only a short distance from the airport where he was a civilian employee. In their early bombing, the planes left two huge craters just across the road from the government apartment building where John lived with his wife and four children. Those bombs also left that apartment building with all the windows shattered.

John had to do something about this situation, but what? The military had ordered all employees in that area to remain in their houses with their families. This apparently was the direction from which they expected a ground attack. The Bengali people were then the buffer between the attacking Freedom Fighters and the West Pakistan controlled airport and military base.

John's intelligence gushed out. One day during curfew he drove up in a roaring camouflaged airport vehicle. He jumped out and said, "Can we come when everything is ready?" Of course the answer was, "Yes, come when you want to."

The next day John slipped away from the airport and brought his two beautiful daughters and some of his more valuable house-hold pieces. The roar of the engine made us wonder how he had been able to get that vehicle away from the airport. Within a few minutes, John called out, "See you tomorrow," and away he roared.

Next he brought his two sons and later his wife. Finally when the airport attacks really got hot, John made his last trip in East Pakistan. He screamed out, "Well, here I am! What are we going to do with this vehicle?" We hid it between the two houses and hoped our side was winning the war. If not, we were in for real trouble.

But people like John made trouble worthwhile. He fled Decca with his family in early 1971. There was no way to support his family; so in May, with his brother-in-law, he started back toward Dacca. They walked 120 miles and then decided to risk a train ride. Shortly after boarding the train, Pakistani soldiers took his brother-in-law away. That was the last John ever saw of him. John had served in the Air Force and, as was true with all Bengali men who served in the armed forces, he learned a West Pakistani language. His ability to speak Punjabi caused the soldiers to think he was a West Pakistani. John's brother-in-law was not so fortunate. John knew what trouble was. He was "lucky" to be alive, and it was good to be associated with people like him.

When we all got settled into the Guest House area, our total number was forty-five — thirty Bengalis and fifteen in our missionary families.

The telephone was still working. Rab Chawdhury called, speaking in an almost indistinguishable voice. I feared greatly for Rab. Following the year's previous tidal wave, he was the relief coordinator for our Noakhali District and some other areas. He and I talked often during the war. We knew that when the army decided to make an all-out attempt to eliminate leading Bengali government officers, he would be among those. In December of 1970, he had refused to "bow" to a West Pakistani Army major. As a result of this, the major had been transferred back to West Pakistan. If that major were back in East Pakistan now, we well knew that Rab was in trouble because of that confrontation and because he was a faithful Bengali.

Rab and I talked briefly on the phone and agreed to keep in touch daily, either by phone, by my going to his home, or by a messenger from him. Of the three Muslim gentlemen whom I admired the most, Rab was the only one with whom I could talk. Mr. Alam, the diplomat turned farmer, was, as far as we knew, still the Foreign Secretary of the Bangladesh government in exile. The professor was a collaborator with the Pakistan army.

So when rumors began spreading that many Bengali government officers were being arrested; I told Betty, "If I ever fail to establish contact with Rab, I will go searching for him and will not return until I have found him or until I know he is dead."

But little rays of hope kept breaking through. Stuart Avery of the New Zealand Baptist Mission was in Dacca with his family. Janet Avery had returned to Dacca with their four children, who had been in a West Pakistan boarding school, only a few days before India became involved in the war. They were not able to go on to their home in Chandpur, so they were with the Phil Parshalls in Dacca. This made it possible for Stuart to bring his children to the Guest House occasionally during the daytime to be with our children. Betty and I were always looking for "help" for our children. The Averys met a real need for us at a desperate time. I watched the children as they talked and played. Though I may

127

have been wrong, it seemed that the Averys had less fear than my children.

Was I just imagining this, or was it true that my keeping my children in the midst of war such a long time had really created problems for them? The evacuation planes still had not been able to land at the Dacca airport. There was opportunity for Betty and the children to prepare again to be evacuated; but after the morning of December 5th, evacuation was never discussed again. This was typical. When we made a decision we felt was right, we put it behind trusting we had decided wisely.

But eventually those evacuation planes came on December 12th. We watched the C-130's of the United States Air Force land quietly at Dacca Airport. Before that day ended, the evacuation was complete.

We didn't have all the facts, but we understood that the only American children left in Dacca were the Thurmans, Debbie Bennett, Lindy Parshall, and ours. Of all other foreign children left, there were the Avery children from New Zealand. I didn't consider these twelve underprivileged. Their parents belonged to organizations which would gladly give the last of their resources to protect them.

Their parents, however, had deep obligations to the people with whom they lived and worked. Even though I was one of the parents, I considered these twelve very fortunate children. I believed the lesson in love would help build them into men and women of strong Christian character.

But for such, there is a price to be paid. As soon as the evacuation planes departed, the war took on a new course. Full scale rocketing and bombing began. It must have been that the Indian Air Force had waited until the foreigners were out of Dacca before they turned on their real strength. The quivering earth told us that the bombs being dropped were larger.

Rumors spread that China was sending planes to aid Pakistan. So the Indian Air Force soon destroyed the runways at the airport by filling it with huge craters to make the Chinese landings impossible.

To me, it was evident — the foreigners were gone; now if necessary, the city could be blasted apart. There would be no international repercussions. This is something of the cheapness of war in Asia. The Bengalis might be blasted into shreds, and little would be said or thought just as it had been for the last nine months.

Around the world there were those few who cared, but they were not the ones who could alter decisions already made.

Obviously, the attacks on Dacca were hastening the day of freedom for the Bengalis. So for this, we as a family were glad; but all principles involving the liberation of Bangladesh had been cast aside. The United States was castigating India for her involvement. But she had been strangely silent during the past nine months about the atrocities being committed by the Pakistanis against the Bengalis. If any objections had been made known, they were so silent we did not hear them.

But the United States did not say too much against Pakistan, for it was Pakistan who arranged Kissinger's secret trip to China during the time of the Freedom Movement. Some of us who saw how Bengalis were being slaughtered in 1971 did not think too highly of Mr. Kissinger's widely acclaimed journey to Peking. In fact, I felt it was the blood of the Bengalis that paid the price of his ticket on Pakistan International Airlines.

Now, of course, China was verbally blasting away at India as if she herself were too moral for any such involvement. The Tibetans and South Koreans gave a different accessment of her morality. And the other big bully, Russia, was also piously sounding off at the United Nations as if she had been invited into Hungary in 1958 and more recently into Czechoslovakia.

We watched during the day and heard and felt during the night as Indian planes continued saturation bombing and rocketing of Pakistan military installations. Bengalis cheered as the planes struck the military targets during the day, but like us, they feared the night.

During the night following the evacuation of the foreigners, the drone of a plane's propelled engines awakened us from our light sleep. The drone increased. There was no doubt the plane was near the Guest House. Then, all of a sudden, the loudest thud we had ever heard, the greatest shaking the Guest House had ever done, frightened us terribly. Within moments another thud, louder, stronger and closer, jerked our house. By the time we had swallowed, a third, with even more force, tore its way into the earth. There was only room for one thought — the next one would get us. The fourth one made us wonder how much a building could take without a direct hit. But then a beautiful sound brought relief. The plane pulled out of its dive and seemingly touched the top of the Guest House's flat roof. It began its way back into the sky. We

129

trembled but gave thanks that we had made it again. The next day, we discovered that the bombs had been dropped a good distance from the Guest House between us and the airport, but it had seemed to us as if it were next door.

Pressure from the Indian planes mounted. They began attacking new areas. One of those was a para-military base about one-quarter mile from the Guest House. The attacking planes flew from East to West over the Intercontinental Hotel, and when they reached our area they were about six hundred feet from the Guest House, to the South. Each time as they were even with the Guest House, we heard a splitting sound and saw a streak of fire as rockets were propelled. Within a few seconds those rockets exploded on or near their target.

Since there were no anti-aircraft guns on this small base, the planes followed the same pattern and attacked again and again. Smoke ascended into the sky as they attacked military groups at Dacca University southeast of the Guest House. When one's nerves were strong, plenty of action was always available from the Guest House.

We received word that all remaining foreigners were permitted to stay at the Intercontinental Hotel which had been declared a neutral zone by the International Red Cross. However we never discussed our going there. The Bengalis with us were not offered that privilege, so what right did we have to it? And hopefully it was apparent that we were not neutral, nor had we been since the brutal plane attack on Feni about eight months before.

A Christian friend, Shova, who was living nearer the airport than we, sent word for me to come. She was living with her three children. I visited her each day since her husband had been transferred to another city by the government. He was a doctor and subject to transfer as often as there was need.

Each time Shova seemed to be doing okay; but eventually she asked me, "Mr. McKinley, is there some way you can get me and the children outside of the city? We are especially afraid at night." She continued, "And the soldiers may come at any time. Without my husband I will have trouble." I checked every possible route but there was no way to get them out of the city. We had even discussed this possibility for ourselves earlier but found that it did not seem practical. I reported to Shova the impossibility. Indian troops and Freedom Fighters were now surrounding the city.

Betty told me to invite Shova and her children to the Guest

House. I did, but she said, "We will just stay here. It is our home. But come as often as you can and see about us." Shova was not the smiling teenage girl we had known when we first moved to Comilla, her home town, in 1959. But like many others, she had gained courage during the past few months. We still, however, felt a deep responsibility to her and her children.

Soon after the evacuation, foreign news broadcasts began telling of a fleet of American ships entering the Bay of Bengal or that section of the Indian ocean. Reportedly, they were making their way toward the port city of Chittagong. We heard many rumors as to why they were coming. One was that they were going to challenge the Indian fleet in the Bay. Another was that they were going to pick up all retreating Pakistan soldiers and take them to West Pakistan so that there would be no slaughter by the advancing Indian and Freedom Fighter Forces. Actually, by this time, thousands of Pakistani soldiers had surrendered in the border areas and were being treated as prisoners of war.

But the crowning reason given was that the ships were coming to evacuate the few remaining Americans in Dacca and other parts of East Pakistan so that they would not be slaughtered by the Bengalis.

This put us in a most dangerous position. The thought of the presence of American planes from aircraft carriers sent Bengali blood boiling. Who were the Americans to be evacuated? We supposed that we must be in the group. But just a few days before, we had passed by an opportunity for evacuation and were told then that this was our last opportunity. We had accepted that. We had no part in such request for evacuation. The thought of American involvement with India in the Bay of Bengal created new fears for us. But we were helpless by-standers watching and listening to the international game of war. We hoped and prayed that those ships were not really entering the Bay.

The early morning of December 14th, our telephone rang. It was a Christian friend, Sudhir Adhikary. Sudhir said, "Mr. McKinley, Rani is sick. Can some arrangement be made to take her to the hospital?" I quickly answered, "Yes, I will come immediately."

But Sudhir said, "There is a curfew. How can it be done?" I replied, "I don't know how, but I'm on my way."

When we lived in Faridpur, Rani was a most attractive and very sweet young lady. She was now married and living about three blocks from the Guest House. Sudhir, her husband, had spoken in a troubled voice over the telephone. There was no objection from Betty and the children as I hurriedly drove out on the vacant street. I stopped a short distance away at a police road block and kept on the offensive by saying, "I'm on my way to the hospital. Will one of you accompany me?" The reply came, "Oh, no, you can make it okay." That's all I wanted, so in a few minutes I drove up to a locked gate.

While the low-flying Indian planes were attacking the paramilitary base nearby, Sudhir came running out. His face, as did all our faces, revealed fear and distress. I asked, "How's Rani?" He replied, "She's coming." Rani didn't look sick — just extremely disturbed. As the planes zoomed over our heads, we hurried over to the brick wall close by.

There Sudhir told the terrible story, "Last night Dr. Siddique Ahmed was taken from our apartment building. I know that I also am on the list to be taken, so can you move us to a safer place? The answer was, "Of course, I can." A Muslim gentleman standing nearby said, "Then will you come take my family?"

We quickly loaded some of their more valuable possessions and made our way to the office of the East Pakistan Christian Council. I breathed a silent prayer for deliverance from road blocks. Sudhir and his family tried to keep out of sight as we moved rapidly. The quietness of the vacant streets felt dangerous.

After unloading their things, Sudhir said, "We may have to move again if our location is discovered." I answered, "Let me know if I need to come."

A few minutes later, I was back at the same apartment house and was glad that my vehicle was a microbus because the Muslim family was large. They quickly piled in some of their possessions as I talked to Mrs. Siddique Ahmed. Mrs. Ahmed was Swedish and seemed so helpless in this land of her husband, who was a scientist.

Mrs. Ahmed asked, "Do you think you could possibly find where they have taken my husband?" I could only answer, "I don't know, but I will try. Please give me his full name and address." Mrs. Ahmed wrote her husband's name on the back of a calling card. She gave me the card, and I promised to contact her as soon as I learned something.

The other family wanted to join relatives on the other side of the city. There was no choice but to take them. We wound through the streets of the old city to places I had never seen. Finally, the

132

gentleman said, "This is it." We banged on a locked gate for several minutes before someone finally peeped out and saw us.

I wished the best for my new friends and made my way to the International Red Cross Office in the Intercontinental Hotel. I passed on the information about Dr. Ahmed. The reply was, "It's been several hours; there isn't much hope of finding him alive, but we will try to contact the army to see if we can learn anything."

Of course, as was now the usual, the army denied any knowledge of Dr. Ahmed. But Mrs. Ahmed learned the next morning that her husband's body had been found. The Razakars, the paramilitary unit collaborating with the army, had worked fast and brutally. Dr. Ahmed's crime, like that of many other Bengalis, was that he was educated, he was a leader and he might give trouble. The next morning Howard Teel moved Mrs. Ahmed into the hotel. She was even then making plans for returning to Sweden as a widow whose husband had been brutally slaughtered.

We no longer wondered what the occasional buses were doing passing the Guest House loaded with blindfolded men during curfew. We now knew it was the brutal Razakars hauling away their Bengali prisoners.

The long night of December 14th gnawed savagely at us. The Indian planes attacked constantly. But added to this was the roar and blasts from the Indian heavy artillery on the outskirts of Dacca.

One blast shook us so much that we found ourselves sitting up under tables talking. We all understood the real danger, but up to this point Wade had not talked much about it. But in the middle of that night, his softly spoken little words brought tears gushing down our cheeks when he asked, "Daddy, will we all be killed?"

I momentarily hesitated and then answered, "Yes, Wade, we may be; but that is not the worst thing that can happen to a family. We love one another, and we are together. We love the Bengalis and they are suffering." It was difficult to say much more. Our emotions were overflowing; but looking back, I feel love was at work. God was very much alive —not in a superficial way, but for real. We felt we somewhat knew Him. We were now involved in a deep struggle. And in that struggle we always found Him.

In the same house little Bapi Sircar grasped his father, Pastor Simon, by the leg and cried out, "Daddy, pray! Daddy, pray!" Boys like Bapi and Wade will be better men because of these difficult times.

133

The Bengali and Indian military forces had Dacca surrounded. Radio reports revealed that there were about 40,000 Pakistani soldiers well fortified in the city. General Niazi, Commander of the Pakistan forces, swore that he would fight to the last man. The American ships were splitting their way through the waters of the Indian Ocean. There were still threats from China to the North. Time was running out.

Dacca was filled with strong ten inch walled buildings. Each floor and roofing of most of those buildings was steel reinforced concrete. Nearly every building was surrounded by strong brick walls. The city buildings provided the rugged Pakistani soldiers with the opportunity of surviving any onslaught of the Bengali and Indian ground attack for weeks, or even as a buffer to protect the soldiers.

With the continuous swearing by General Niazi to fight to the last man, we expected rough days leading up to Christmas and on into the new year. I wondered — were we emotionally and spiritually prepared for such a struggle?

We constantly listened to various short-wave radio broadcasts. We had heard the news clearly telling of the advance of the Indian and Bengali forces. Each day, we knew their distance from Dacca. On the morning of December 15th we heard, "The Indian Army has the city of Dacca surrounded. Their planes control the air. General Niazi continues to say he will fight to the last man to hold the city."

Such news caused us to tremble. Though thousands had left Dacca in early December, it was estimated that possibly up to 200,000 people were still in the city with no way out.

But we were also sure that since we were hearing these short-wave broadcasts, our friends around the world had the same news. Neither we nor these estimated 200,000 Bengalis were forgotten. Though often we were so low we hardly felt like praying, we knew strong friends were praying.

During the few times of December 15th when the planes were not attacking, there was absolute silence except the bursting of shells on the periphery of the city. There weren't many smiles on our faces. That night it was rather quiet. Only the sounds from planes bombing the army areas north of the airport troubled us.

We had heard rumors that Pakistan was going to surrender, but I didn't believe the Muslim Army had reached the point when

134

it was ready to surrender to an army dominated by Indian Hindus. From what I knew of the city, before India and the Bengalis could take it, the Pakistan army was in a position to kill two or even three of their opposition before one of their own men died.

On the early morning of December 16th, I climbed the steps leading to the flat roof of the Guest House. Only one Indian plane was in the sky. The burst of shells could be heard and smoke seen in the distance, but the city was not being attacked. It seemed that this was the calm before the storm.

But thanks to God I was wrong. We were sitting in the death trap, but the radio news said, "General Niazi has been ordered to surrender his forces in East Pakistan." With that statement, there was no more East Pakistan to anyone.

Suddenly, we saw — we experienced, the birth of a giant nation — the world's eighth largest in population. Bangladesh, the nation of the Bengalis was born. And we felt like one of them.

Within an hour's time, hundreds of fully armed Pakistan soldiers came from every direction and moved north up the road by the Guest House toward the army base to surrender to the Indian Army. We had no idea that so many of them had been in hiding near us waiting for the arrival of their would be attackers.

The Pakistani soldiers' heads drooped low as they dragged their feet. For thirteen days, they had been under heavy attacks from the air. Most of them had had little sleep. They seemed hardly able to carry their rifles. From this problem, some of them received help as Bengali young men ran out into the streets and pulled at their rifles. Some of them handed the rifles to the Bengalis.

Within that same hour, the Bengali and Indian soldiers poured into the city. The first main entrance into the city was from the west down the road by our Guest House. So we were in the welcoming group. The Bengalis went wild. Everywhere we looked, there were people carrying rifles, firing them wildly into the air. Some little boys had to drag theirs, for they were too heavy to carry.

Some young men ran past the Guest House changing clothes as they ran. We knew they were the Razakars, who had collaborated with the army. They were quickly trying to change their appearance.

The police vacated the station just south of the Guest House, since some of them had been collaborators. Civilians ransacked

135

the station carrying away pistols, rifles and other weapons as well as boxes of shells.

Though we sensed a new danger, we too, were caught up in the excitement of freedom. Our children, along with Debbie Bennett, the Thurman boys and the Bengali children, stood by the gate waving wildly to the victorious soldiers as they continued to enter the city.

Gloria Thurman helped Cherie and Kathy make a Bangladesh flag. We raised it on top of the Guest House. But even before that, the first flag we saw in free Bangladesh was one that Marj Bennett pulled out of hiding as soon as the surrender was announced. The children, standing by the gate, drew wild applause when the little flag was seen.

Indian soldiers stopped by the Guest House to inquire who we were and if we were okay. Bangladesh was free. That was all that counted right then.